T0143697

THE LAST BLUE MOUNTAIN

ALSO BY RALPH BARKER:

Down in the Drink
The Ship-Busters
Strike Hard, Strike Sure
Ten Great Innings
The Thousand Plan
Great Mysteries of the Air
Ten Great Bowlers
Aviator Extraordinary
Test Cricket, England v Australia 1877–1968 (with Irving Rosenwater)
Verdict on a Lost Flyer
The Schneider Trophy Races
Against the Sea
One Man's Jungle
Survival in the Sky
The Blockade Busters
The Cricketing Family Edrich
The Hurricats
Not Here, But in Another Place
Innings of a Lifetime
Goodnight, Sorry for Sinking You
Children of the Benares
Purple Patches
That Eternal Summer
The Royal Flying Corps in France, Parts I and II
A Brief History of the Royal Flying Corps in World War I
The RAF at War
Men of the Bombers

THE
THE GREAT

LAST
KARAKORAM

BLUE
CLIMBING

MOUNTAIN
TRAGEDY

RALPH BARKER

Vertebrate Publishing, Sheffield
www.v-publishing.co.uk

'We are the Pilgrims, master; we shall go
Always a little further: it may be
Beyond that last blue mountain barred with snow … '

James Elroy Flecker

THE LAST BLUE MOUNTAIN

RALPH BARKER

First published in 1959 by Chatto and Windus.
This edition first published in 2020 by Vertebrate Publishing.

VP Vertebrate Publishing
Omega Court, 352 Cemetery Road, Sheffield S11 8FT, United Kingdom.
www.v-publishing.co.uk

© Ralph Barker 1959.
Foreword © Lord Hunt 1959.
Introduction © Ed Douglas 2020.
'The Runcible Cat' © John Emery. First published in the *Alpine Journal* in 1961.

Front cover photo: Haramosh peak. © Najmul Hassan/Getty Images.
All other photographs and illustrations courtesy of the Streather family.

Ralph Barker has the right under the Copyright, Designs and Patents Act 1988
to be identified as author of this work.

This book is a work of non-fiction based on the life, diaries and recollections of
Rae Culbert, John Emery, Scott Hamilton, Bernard Jillott and Tony Streather.

A CIP catalogue record for this book is available from the British Library.

ISBN: 978-1-912560-42-4 (Paperback)
ISBN: 978-1-912560-43-1 (Ebook)
ISBN: 978-1-912560-44-8 (Audiobook)

10 9 8 7 6 5 4 3 2 1

All rights reserved. No part of this book covered by the copyright herein may
be reproduced or used in any form or by any means – graphic, electronic,
or mechanised, including photocopying, recording, taping or information
storage and retrieval systems – without the written permission of the publisher.

Every effort has been made to obtain the necessary permissions with
reference to copyright material, both illustrative and quoted. We apologise
for any omissions in this respect and will be pleased to make the appropriate
acknowledgements in any future edition.

Cover design by Jane Beagley, typesetting by Cameron Bonser,
Vertebrate Publishing.
www.v-publishing.co.uk

CONTENTS

INTRODUCTION TO THE 2020 EDITION

Several years ago, I sat in a London crown court listening to a barrister explain to a judge what it was like to be trapped high on a big mountain in the Himalaya in worsening weather, making decisions that would impact not just on one person's safety but that of a whole team in circumstances of extreme physical hardship and danger. Even after a good night's rest at sea level, he argued, the brain could be a fickle mechanism. Was it possible to pass judgement on one fatigued by days of effort with minimal rest?

Gradually the court was hushed as the barrister filled out the picture of his client's situation: the strengthening wind, the snow stinging his face, the fight for breath, the numbing of feet and hands, the psychological pressure of a remote situation, far from the help of others. We were no longer in London but high in the Himalaya, in desperate trouble. I was startled to feel the hairs on the back of my neck prickle with fear and almost laughed: up until then, I thought that was simply a figure of speech.

After the day's proceedings, I asked a friendly solicitor if the barrister was a climber. He seemed to understand viscerally the situation he was describing; he must have been in similar situations himself. The solicitor laughed. 'Him? I'm not sure he ever leaves the city, let alone climbs mountains.' What I'd heard was simply a supreme act of the imagination, the ability to think through the consequences of such a hostile environment on a weary, desperate and vulnerable human being, and communicate that experience with a simple intensity that was almost unbearable.

Ralph Barker did something similar in *The Last Blue Mountain*, his memorable account of an attempt in 1957 by a group mostly of students from Oxford University on the Karakoram peak of Haramosh, an adventure that ended in a protracted and ultimately fatal misadventure whose twists and turns heaped agonies on top of each other. That anyone survived it at all is testament to the courage, resilience and good luck of the two who escaped: the medical student John Emery, and the soldier Tony Streather, an experienced hand brought in to win approval for the enterprise. Streather's ascent of Kangchenjunga two years earlier had made him something of a celebrity. Barker's version of their story, told for a general audience, is in the same genre as Joe Simpson's *Touching the Void*, now a much more famous book, which in the 1980s helped reinvigorate a similar strand of narrative non-fiction that Barker was drawing on at the end of the 1950s. Think of Paul Brickhill's *The Great Escape*.

Joe Simpson of course was his own subject, had lived through his own epic and could look hard into his own soul for the meaning and direction of the story he was telling. Ralph Barker hadn't been on Haramosh or any other mountain; like the barrister in court he had to rely on his own imagination, judgement and empathy to unravel the contrasting motivations and personalities of the climbers and the complex sequence of events on the mountain. The first three-quarters of *The Last Blue Mountain* moves along crisply, setting the scene, offering concise portraits of the climbers and their mountain; but it is all preparation and context for the intense conclusion as these climbers we have come to know and like are faced with unimaginable odds. The book's great strength is the way Barker, without ever drifting from his fast-paced narrative, shows how character and fate intertwine.

Some aspects now feel a little dated. It is unquestionably a male book: inevitably given that all the protagonists are men. And the author does on a few occasions dip into language that will make some modern readers flinch a little. But despite how tight-lipped 1950s England was supposed to have been, Barker had a liberal rein to use diaries and letters to lift the tough carapace on these men and expose a more complex version of themselves: their frailties as well as their strengths. He does this with an unfailing sympathy that prevents him from being too abrupt in his judgements. Men have died, and he is respectful of the loss others have suffered. If mistakes were made, then they were understandable and are more than offset by the sacrifice and courage of all involved. It is this combination of openness and respect that has secured the book's survival, as much as its thrilling tale.

All the protagonists are well drawn: the hugely likeable Kiwi Rae Culbert, the not-so-quiet American Scott Hamilton and the impressive John Emery. (All those I have spoken to about Emery, all old men now, speak of him with great fondness and respect.) But Barker zeroes in, correctly I think, on the differences between the expedition's leader, Tony Streather, an Army officer with immense stamina, and the project's driving force, an ambitious young climber from Huddersfield, 'very much of the Buhl temperament', called Bernard Jillott, whose climbing partners at Oxford included the young educationalist Colin Mortlock. Streather had come to prominence in a series of expeditions to big mountains, starting with the first ascent of Tirich Mir in Chitral, where he had 'stayed on' after independence and the risks he faced daily on the frontier gave him a depth of experience that his teammates, who weren't *that* much younger, couldn't possibly match. He loved Pakistan, and the expedition to Haramosh was an opportunity to renew friendships. He also understood the Hunza men who worked as porters on the expedition, their limitations and expectations, in a way that Jillott, who was driven and impulsive, did not. These two, with such different backgrounds and temperaments, would chafe against each other.

Barker may not have had experience of mountains but he understood men under pressure. After a stint on the *Sporting Life*, he had gone into banking before joining the RAF. He served as a wireless operator and gunner in a Beaufort torpedo bomber squadron attacking Axis shipping in the Mediterranean that was resupplying Rommel's Panzers in the Western Desert: a notoriously risky occupation in such an unreliable aircraft. When Barker's crashed, killing the pilot and navigator, he returned to Britain and spent the rest of the war flying transport aircraft.

Demobbed in 1946, Barker struggled to find meaningful work and consequently re-enlisted in the RAF two years later. He was sent to Berlin during the airlift as a press officer and spent a few more years in Germany with the British Forces Network before returning to work on official war narratives at the Air Ministry. What he learned there would nourish his later career as a full-time writer. A chance remark from a colleague about the Goldfish Club, founded to reunite those serving airmen who had crash-landed 'in the drink' and survived, gave him the idea for his first book. His next described the wartime role of the torpedo bomber squadrons he had served.

How Barker swerved from military history to write *The Last Blue Mountain*, his third book and on an entirely new subject, is something of a mystery. Bernard Jillott, Barker tells us, was planning to write a book, so perhaps Barker inherited this project. Perhaps his military service made the connection with Streather, but that is simply a guess. Why the climbers trusted him is also intriguing. There was, and to some extent remains, a deep-seated antipathy among climbers to non-climbing third parties writing about mountaineering tragedies. In later life Barker concentrated on military aviation, survival and his other great passion, cricket, which he played for Adastrians, a team for ex-RAF servicemen, and El Vino's. He died aged ninety-three in 2011.

Of course, Barker's version of this extraordinary expedition is simply that: a version, albeit a compelling one. As someone who has also written about other people's mountaineering tragedies, I'm only too aware that for a general audience in particular, even a well-informed one, narratives are sometimes simplified, or someone's strongly held views contradicted. When John Emery, having qualified as a doctor despite suffering appalling amputations to his hands and feet, died in a fall from the Weisshorn in 1963 aged just twenty-nine, his obituarist in the *Climbers' Club Journal* observed that the best account of the Haramosh expedition had come from Emery's own lips. None of which detracts from this classic of climbing literature: it is an epic story well told.

Accuracy is one thing, truth another. The title of the book, *The Last Blue Mountain*, was the suggestion of Tony Streather's wife Sue. The phrase is drawn from the final lines of James Elroy Flecker's play *Hassan* and spoken by a pilgrim; it captures the romance of mountaineering. (An earlier phrase from the same verse, 'Always a little further', was the title for Alastair Borthwick's classic memoir of climbing in Scotland in the 1930s.) The closing lines of the play, however, add a more thoughtful perspective. The watchman at the gate the pilgrims have just passed through tries to console the women who watch them go. 'What would ye, ladies?' he says. 'It was ever thus. / Men are unwise and curiously planned.' One of the women then says: 'They have their dreams, and do not think of us.' Except that Tony Streather spent long days in his tent on Haramosh, sheltering from the foul Karakoram weather, thinking of Sue and their young son, and questioning the wisdom of their enterprise and the choices they had made. Such questions would haunt him until his death, aged ninety-two, in 2018.

Ed Douglas

FOREWORD TO THE 1959 EDITION

We are living in an age which, more than ever, judges an enterprise by the tangible result; judged by this yardstick the attempt by British climbers on Haramosh in 1957 was a tragic failure. That those who reach their goal and return safely have, in an immediate and obvious sense, succeeded is not disputed; but what of others who make the journey without, in the analogy of Cervantes, reaching the inn? What of the Polar party in 1912, and of Mallory and Irvine on Everest in 1924? Did these men, and many others, necessarily fail?

The matter deserves a deeper scrutiny. The true result of endeavour, whether on a mountain or in any other context, may be found rather in its lasting effects than in the few moments during which a summit is trampled by mountain boots. The real measure is the success or failure of the climber to triumph not over a lifeless mountain but over himself: the true value of the enterprise lies in the example to others of human motive and human conduct.

Accidents are never to be sought in mountaineering. I am not encouraging them by saying that the greatness of this sport rests mainly in the risk of their happening. If we ever succeed in making climbing safe from danger, we had better give it up for something which retains the element of hazard. When an accident occurs, something may emerge of lasting value, for the human spirit may rise to its greatest heights. This happened on Haramosh.

From this truer viewpoint, this story is not one of failure but of triumph.

Lord Hunt KG, CBE, DSO

Leader of the British expedition to Everest in 1953 and author of *The Ascent of Everest*

AUTHOR'S NOTE

To write the story of an expedition of this kind is to feel the growth of a deep admiration and affection for the men who took part in it. To be entrusted with such a task was a great privilege. I was allowed to see and study the personal diaries of the climbers, in which from day to day they recorded their innermost thoughts about the expedition, about each other, and about themselves. I was able to discuss every aspect of the expedition with two of the survivors, and to correspond fully with a third.

I would like the reader to know of and share my admiration for their courage in deciding, within a few weeks of their tragic and terrible experience, that a non-mountaineer, unknown to any member of the expedition, should tell their story.

Ralph Barker

1

HARAMOSH

It had been easy, back in England, contemplating the Himalaya from a distance, with the bigger peaks of Everest, K2 and Kangchenjunga jutting into their minds, to think of their mountain, the 24,270-foot Haramosh, as being something within their compass, a mountain just about their size. And even now, as they camped in the hairpin arena of the high Kutwal Valley, 11,000 feet above sea level, hemmed in on all sides by mountains like a monstrous dry-dock, it was impossible to realise that facing them, a mile across the boulder-strewn Mani glacier, the north face of Haramosh, four miles long, soared and tumbled a further 13,000 feet into the sky.

Confronted by such a giant, surrounded by its kind if not by its equals, one's eye had no point of reference with remembered heights.

To Bernard Jillott, twenty-three-year-old organiser and deputy leader of the expedition, it seemed that some of those rock ridges that crinkled up from the base of the mountain like the pleats of a skirt might be climbed in a morning, before the sun loosened the chaotic ice cliffs that overhung every inch of the north face and sent avalanches of snow and ice billowing down the mountainside on to the glacier, destroying anything that loitered in their path. His mountaineer's eye, unaccustomed to the Himalaya, saw the problem momentarily on an Alpine scale. He ran his eye up the most prominent ridge until it reached the forehead of ice cliffs below the summit. It looked a climb of 3,000 feet, no more. But from the known height of the summit above the valley it must be about 8,000 feet, needing at least three camps on the ridge itself, each one of which would be swept away from above almost before it was pitched.

And yet it looked easy. It seemed that the eye, like the camera lens, could not focus on so immense a subject without taking a metaphorical step back to get the whole in its aperture, reducing it as it did so to snapshot size.

For Jillott, the sight of Haramosh piling up in front of him was very much more than a challenge, real and urgent as the challenge was. It was the fulfilment of an ambition that had been conceived more than a year earlier, in 1956, when he was still president of the Oxford University Mountaineering Club. It was the realisation, though, of very much more than a single ambition. It was the fulfilment of his whole being.

Although tall and lithe, he had never been much of an athlete at school. In his work, of course, he had always been top, right through his grammar school days. Never anything but first. He got used to it and he liked it. But he had had no ability or zest for team games, and this coupled with his superiority as a scholar had tended to isolate him. An only child, inclined to be quiet and shy, he did not make friends easily. The only game he played well was tennis, which suited his liking for a personal struggle. He relished the opportunity for short, sharp conquest, complete in itself, that each point offered.

Exercise and companionship, and the beauty of mountain scenery, had been his early incentives to climb. At school he had organised parties to the Lake District, walking rather than climbing, and these episodes had become more and more important to him. Then, during National Service in the Army, stationed at Inverness, he had started rock climbing. Soon he was getting an elation from success in a hard climb that nothing else in life had ever given him.

When he won his scholarship to Oxford, he had joined the mountaineering club. He had given all his spare time to climbing. It had become a religion. He began to attempt the more difficult rock climbs. Soon he was making a name for himself. He was impatient to attempt new routes, to solve fresh problems, to know the explorer's excitement in untrodden ways.

He discovered that climbing, supposedly non-competitive, could be among the most keenly competitive of sports. Soon he had two Alpine first ascents to his credit. He began to hear his name mentioned as one of the most promising rock climbers in the country. There was only one major field in which he was still untested – the Himalaya. It was inevitable that thoughts of an expedition – his own expedition, but with an experienced Himalayan climber invited to lead – should press themselves upon him.

It was then that he had thought of Tony Streather. To get the right backing for his expedition, moral and financial, he must capture some big name in mountaineering as leader. Yet he had to choose a man whose approach to climbing was essentially amateur – someone who would be interested in taking a small expedition to an unclimbed but little-known peak just for the fun of it, without the publicity which accompanied a big expedition to a famous mountain.

Streather, he had decided, would satisfy both these requirements. He was without doubt in the very front rank as a Himalayan climber. He had climbed Tirich Mir with the Norwegians in 1950, and had been with the Americans on K2 in 1953, standing up to the disastrous fall better than almost anyone else, and subsequently helping to lead the exhausted party down. In 1955 he had gone to the top of Kangchenjunga, then the highest unclimbed peak in the world, inferior in height only to Everest and K2. And as a regular Army officer, his amateur approach to climbing was sure. The shunning of publicity and heroics would be ingrained in him.

These were the sort of thoughts that had passed through Jillott's mind during the summer of 1956. He had sought advice at Oxford on the possibility of gaining support for a University expedition, combining the mapping and exploration of a little-known area with the scaling of a significant peak. From several suggested possibilities he had selected Haramosh, mainly because of its accessibility. Although Haramosh was nearly a thousand miles north-east of Karachi, they could travel by air as far as Gilgit, forty miles west of Haramosh, leaving a day's ride by Jeep to the road-head at Sussi and then two days on foot to the Kutwal Valley and the Mani glacier. They could encompass the journey, the survey, and a worthwhile attempt at an ascent, in the long vacation.

Jillott had invited Streather to Oxford to talk to the mountaineering club about K2, and he had broached the subject after the lecture. Streather was just the sort of man he had expected – modest and reserved but free from shyness or diffidence, tremendously compact, and exuding physical and mental fitness. For all Streather's gentle manner there was an unmistakable vitality and robustness about him. His reaction to Jillott's proposal had been one of quiet but genuine interest, and Jillott was enormously encouraged. He felt at once that he could take Streather at his word.

Then there was the question of finding a team. Jillott's years in mountaineering had changed him from an unknown young man with few friends to a popular climber with many. Modest and unassuming, he had a great ability for getting on with people. Even so, in the choice of his team he was restricted to those members of the mountaineering club who could find both the money and the time. Each member of the team was asked to subscribe £100 to the expedition fund.

Eventually he settled on five men: Streather and himself; Rae Culbert, a twenty-five-year-old New Zealander; John Emery, a twenty-three-year-old medical student from St Mary's Hospital, Paddington; and Scott Hamilton, an American from Little Rock, Arkansas. All apart from

Streather were fellow members of the OUMC and personal friends with whom Jillott had climbed.

He had set about the preparatory organisation with what had seemed at the time to be inexhaustible energy and enthusiasm. Throughout the early months of 1956 he had been working hard for his finals, and then had followed a year's concentrated research. But the mass of detail necessary to the planning of such an expedition was meticulously attended to. By October 1956, plans were ready for submission to the Pakistan Government, without whose permission the expedition would be stillborn. Then there was the money side. The blessing of the Oxford University expedition council was needed, since the magic name of the University meant everything to their requests for financial support. With it, they could hope for a sizeable grant from the Everest Foundation. He remembered now the thrill of pleasure and relief when the Foundation's promise of help to the tune of £1,200 was made.

Other grants, coupled with book and press contracts, and the generosity of manufacturers in giving supplies of their goods, had more than covered their original budget, so that, apart from Emery, who had accompanied the baggage by sea, they had eventually been able to fly out, saving a commodity even more precious to them than money – time. Streather had only two months' leave from Sandhurst, where he was an instructor, and the whole expedition had to be accomplished in this time.

But the last few months before the scheduled departure date had been agonising. The most shattering of many frustrations had come when the Commonwealth Relations Office in London had informed them of the Pakistan Government's refusal to admit an expedition this year. Financial worries had beset them throughout, right up to the signing of the press contract. There had been the doubts raised by the stalemate in the Kashmir dispute. It had been many months before Streather had finally been able to confirm that he could come – and until his name could be put at the head of the climbing party it had been no use writing to anybody. Then had come the Suez crisis. Short of time as they were bound to be, the blocking of the Canal meant that they would have to sail round the Cape, a delay that was almost insupportable. It was only at the last minute that the press contract had enabled them to travel by air.

Jillott had borne the brunt of all these frustrations; and although the Pakistan Government had been prevailed upon to change their mind, and all their other difficulties had somehow been resolved, towards the end the keenness of his enthusiasm had been blunted. He was apt to be intolerant of anything that interfered with his plans; and he had been tempted to change his plans altogether rather than endure these endless frustrations. Other climbing friends had made up a party to go to Norway, and at one point he decided that if Haramosh was going to be as tantalising as this, he would give up the whole idea and go to Norway.

But the merest reference to such a possibility had excited such disapproval from the others, all of whom were now determined to go to the Himalaya this year, that he had had to retract at once. He had started something that he couldn't possibly abandon. The momentum of the expedition, which he himself had begun and largely helped to accelerate, was too great for him to jump off now.

Besides, it was *his* expedition, a stupendous achievement, and he must stand by it. This dull feeling was only reaction from his strenuous efforts at work and play of the last three years. Once the expedition was underway, the old excitement would return.

And, of course, so it had. Although he had suffered a bad attack of dysentery on the way up from Gilgit, sufficient to delay him for two days, together with John Emery as doctor, he felt fit now and intensely stimulated by the challenge of the mountain before him.

He couldn't quite put his finger on what it was that gave him the terrific boost he got from climbing. He knew that it would always be the first thing in his life. It dwarfed everything else – home, education, ambition. The hills were home, education was a means to an end, something that would ultimately give him the time and opportunity to climb. That was his only ambition. Everything in life he would subordinate to it. He knew that such singleness of purpose on such an issue might be censured. But he was used to having his way.

At first he had tried to keep his passion for climbing from his parents, but inevitably it had come out. He was not of a secretive nature and, although he disliked hurting them, or indeed anyone or anything, he had been glad when they knew. His mother had done everything to dissuade him, naturally enough, since he was the focus of her life and of his father's. Their last battle had been just before he left home for Haramosh.

His mind went back to that last day, saying goodbye to his family at his Yorkshire home. Everyone had come to see him off. He hadn't known how the sunlight had glinted on his fair hair, how they had caught him in an unguarded moment looking away into something remote that they had known they would never see. He had seemed to be looking beyond this world altogether. All he had been aware of was his mother's last entreaty, still troubling his conscience.

'There's nothing I can say to stop you, Bernard, is there?'

'I'm afraid not, Mother.'

'When are you going to give it up?'

That was something he knew he would never be able to do.

'People still climb at sixty. Even older than that. I shall always climb.'

He knew that his mother was baffled, perplexed, hurt by his intractability. He wanted desperately to explain it to her, to make her understand.

'When I'm on the mountain, something happens to me inside.' He spoke slowly, and with a sort of wonder. 'I know an exhilaration that's past all describing. It's a part of me. I can't change now.'

For almost the whole of its five-mile length, the Kutwal Valley was dominated by the hideous beauty of the north face of Haramosh, rising almost sheer in tumbled masses of glittering ice, in intricate complexities of pinnacles and ridges and gullies and hanging glaciers, topped by the long line of ice cliffs, and emerging at either end into a well-defined summit. The ice cliffs formed the chain which linked the twin peaks – Haramosh II towards the head of the valley, and Haramosh I to their right. This was the challenging peak, leaning a little back from the valley, and even from its own terrible precipices, almost as though it didn't have much of a head for heights.

But as the mountain crept to its highest point, it pursed itself, and smoothed its contours, suddenly conscious, like a mountaineer, of the approach of the moment of truth. The slopes up to the foot of the final cone were smooth and feminine. So vast was the scale that Haramosh II, four miles distant towards the head of the valley, was its natural twin.

To stand in this narrow gorge of a valley, and to feel the propinquity of mountains – facing one, beside one and at one's back – was to pull the Himalaya round one like a cloak. A cloak of ebony and white. These were the Karakoram mountains, the north-west part of the Himalaya, and Karakoram meant 'black rock', a hardy rock that stood straight and sheer and refused to be wholly clothed by snow. They were harsh mountains but there was poetry in their grandeur.

John Emery, the young medical student, was himself a mixture of poet and mountaineer. The climber in him saw the mountain as an inanimate thing, something with which he would be grappling for the next six or seven weeks. But the poet in him recognised the beauty of Haramosh.

Like Jillott an only child, Emery had experienced the closer contacts of boarding school and was more deeply involved with his fellow men. He had a highly developed critical faculty, to the point of fastidiousness, but he was quick and generous in his admiration. He was perhaps the only one of the party capable of feeling that depth of affection for another man which amounts to love. Others in the party might develop it, but in John Emery it was already there.

Younger than Jillott in many ways, he had started climbing later and therefore developed later. He was now just about Jillott's equal, and the two men climbed together with tremendous rhythm and purpose. Even so, Emery had never quite forgotten that Jillott had once been ahead of him, and he still looked upon him as the senior partner. But emotionally and aesthetically Emery was the more mature person. Jillott, he knew, had little time for women. But Emery, warm and affectionate by nature, was easily involved. Although he had felt attracted to several women, none of them had seriously vied with climbing as his first love. Not, anyway, until the voyage out from England.

At sea, travelling with the ton or more of expedition stores, Emery had been completely dissociated from reality. Events past and future seemed to lose all significance, and he had existed in a vacuum, a charming and fairyland present. Everything near seemed to be magnified by its sheer proximity; everything distant seemed impossibly remote. Then for the first time he had seen something which seemed to him to be perfection in a woman. The attachment that resulted was one which for various reasons could not possibly develop beyond its context, but he had sensed that her feelings for him were more than mere friendship. It had been a significant experience for both of them, he was sure, and not a mere shipboard flirtation. They were constantly together, and they had been amongst the happiest hours of his life.

His first few days in Pakistan had been almost unbearable. He could not share the enthusiasm of the rest of the party, although he was as keen to get to the mountain as they were; and for the moment he had a strange feeling of being outside the expedition, watching it as a spectator. Soon he would shake this off, but for the moment it was hard to find a meeting point with anyone. He could not talk about the woman from the ship yet, but he could concentrate on nothing else. Jillott wasn't interested in women anyway, so he couldn't talk to him. Scott Hamilton, good-natured and voluble as ever, suddenly seemed trivial and immature. He thought he might talk about it later with Tony Streather, but Streather's calm self-sufficiency was a barrier for the moment. Only Rae Culbert's quietly delivered witticisms, often broad and debunking in tone, were in tune with his mood.

Then, in Sussi, with only two days' march ahead before they reached Haramosh, Jillott had gone down with dysentery, and as expedition doctor Emery had had to stay behind in Sussi to treat him while the others went on. At last Jillott had been fit enough to walk the twenty miles to the Kutwal Valley. There had followed two days of suffocating heat, of dust-laden throats, of constant consideration for a still half-sick man. He began to understand why people quickly became impatient with the illness of others. But his own patience was fortified by Jillott's determination to press on in spite of the debilitating effects of the dysentery.

And at every village Emery had been reminded of the duty he had accepted by studying medicine, so that he could never be completely carefree. There they sat, rows and rows of apathetic but exasperatingly patient villagers, determined to be cured by the 'Doctor Sahib'. To him they were an insidious personal reproach and an indictment of his calling.

He could see that they would wait for ever, and that he could almost treat them for ever. What did one do? Tell them, ninety-five per cent of them, that they were chronically diseased and that there was nothing a medical student and a box of pills could do for them? Or hand out a pill here and there and hope that faith might work miracles? What a mockery they had made of his first-class honours! And how irritable he had felt with them, and even more so with himself, because he knew how unworthy it had been. He had been obsessed with the idea of reaching the mountain and starting the climb, to scarify his being against the rugged mountain.

So climbing this time was to be an escape. Or was it? He had always argued that it gave him perspective, a self-awareness, a reassessment of values. Perhaps once on the mountain he would be able to relate the deep emotional experience that still lay heavy on him to the larger scheme of things.

Climbing had always done that for him. Difficulties had piled up: exams, the hospital, people; and he had always known that he could go to the hills and step out of life's abrasive underwear, feeling a great sense of release and freedom. In the same way that, as you gained height, the immediate topography fell into perspective, so did the world of the mind.

Worry, disappointment, dissatisfaction – all fell away when you were on, say, the last leg of an ice climb in mid-winter, faced with thirty feet of vertical ice, with perhaps only an hour's daylight left. It was blowing a gale, snow was pouring down the pitch on to your face, and halfway up you felt that all your strength was leaving you, your arms and your legs were limp, you didn't know how to go on. It was a stark and personal struggle with the elements and with yourself. Trivialities dropped away, you found untapped reserves of strength and willpower you hardly knew you possessed, you overcame the physical difficulties of the climb, and you conquered the weakness of self. The elation when you'd done it was like a shot of adrenalin. You felt pulsatingly alive.

You went back to your problems to find them sorry creatures, easily disposed of. You were the master of yourself again, not the easy prey to idle fears. You had wrested from the mountain something of its own inviolability and peace. Like the mountain, you were satisfied just to be.

And to add to all this, and to intensify each part of it, was the comradeship. That was something the sense of which he'd lost for the moment, but it would return. It was the most solid, the deepest thing of all. Up there on the mountain you faced the ultimate danger. There was no sense in denying it; that was what lent the magic to it. Anyway, that was how it was for him. People called mountaineering a sport. It wasn't a sport for him. The difference was fundamental.

One felt a bond with those with whom one had fought a winning or losing game of rugger, soccer, hockey, cricket – the bond of shared ability, physical effort, the fluctuations of fortune, adversity, victory and defeat. But the strongest bond was that of the danger shared, strongest of all when that danger was the ultimate one. He imagined that it might be indistinguishable from the bond of danger shared in battle.

This was the bond he shared with Bernard Jillott. He had spent two seasons climbing with Jillott in the Alps, and they had climbed together a lot in Wales, the Lakes and in Scotland. He knew Jillott as a bold and determined climber and leader, absolutely trustworthy and returning his trust, a man who only gave up if the odds were overwhelmingly against him.

Jillott was a beautiful mover on rock, and tremendously sure. Emery had never seen anyone move with quite such skill and confidence as Jillott on that last weekend together in Wales. He was just as good on the granite of the Alps, though perhaps not quite so sound on snow and ice. Emery guessed that Jillott might not always be aware of his own limitations, few as they were, and that he might sometimes be bold almost to the point of rashness, but this suited his own climbing temperament.

As with Jillott, it was the sense of personal combat, personal achieve- ment, that Emery looked for in climbing. He shared Jillott's enthusiasm for games which involved the conflict of individuals: his half-blue had been for fencing, another of his interests was boxing. Artistically minded, and highly literate, he yet preferred the sports and pastimes which offered risk of physical injury. Jillott, he felt, sought to demonstrate his ability not so much to others as to himself. He was not an exhibitionist. But, whatever the reason, they were both almost rapacious where mountains were concerned. To see one was to desire to conquer it.

Yet, outside of mountaineering, they were utterly unlike in temper- ament, and indeed knew each other very little. Although Emery had known that Jillott was planning this Himalayan venture, it was only as a result of a chance meeting with him on a visit to Oxford from St Mary's the previous October that his invitation had come. One of Jillott's original choices had backed out, Streather had said that the party ought to include a doctor, and Jillott had invited Emery.

'It's a wonderful thought,' Emery had said. 'But I don't suppose I've got much chance of getting away.'

'Won't Mary's let you go?'

'I've got my finals in September next year. I couldn't very well be away half the summer.'

'Couldn't you put them back a few months?'

'I'll see what they say. I'll certainly have a shot at it. I'd love to come.'

'I'll hold the place for you. Let me know as soon as you can.'

Back at Mary's, he had felt like putting off the moment when he must ask the question as long as possible, since the answer could only be no, and he wanted to dream about it a little longer. But he had gone to see the secretary of the medical school at once. He had told his story, and then waited for the dream to dissolve under the hard light of Paddington.

'The great thing about Mary's,' the secretary was saying, 'is that when you want to do something really worthwhile, we encourage you in its pursuit.'

So far he was still dreaming.

'You say you want three months' leave. That means putting back your finals.'

The dream was dissolving and he saw that his horizon for a long time was going to be St Mary's.

'I'm sure that can be arranged. When do you want to go?'

It couldn't be as easy as this. 'I suppose some time in July.'

'Write to the Dean. I'll mention it to him meanwhile. I should think he'll very probably let you go.'

And the Dean had given him the three months' leave he'd asked for, plus an extra month to get fit!

The extra time had meant that he had been able to take on the job of accompanying the expedition stores by ship. He'd done his best to get fit before he left England, but the softening process of the sea voyage had changed all that. Now he was just about as unfit as he could possibly be. The only solution was to get to grips with the mountain.

The sea voyage was something that with time he might remember with tenderness. As yet, the pain was too acute and he must exorcise it from his memory. Love was of the valley, Tennyson had said. The mountain would set him free.

2

IN THE KUTWAL VALLEY

The head of the Kutwal Valley was the apex of a lengthy gorge that had
elbowed its way between the mountains all the way up from Sussi,
climbing nearly 6,000 feet on the way. And from the Kutwal Valley they
could look back along their tracks, down the winding gorge, watching the
ground fall away until the shoulders of the hills abutted and hid the gorge
from view.

All the way from Sussi they had trudged uphill over bare, sandy earth,
in stifling heat, lashed by a hot gusting wind. Occasionally, at the
villages, there had been patches of irrigation, but these had been few.
Dust and sand and the smell of ordure had clogged their throats and
nostrils. Once or twice, as they climbed above the river, or where the
path plunged into a ravine, they had caught a sudden cool rush of air,
smelling sweetly of the high pastures; and once, by a rickety bridge
across the gorge, there were tamarisks in full bloom. But the enervating
cauldron of the gorge had been oppressively with them almost till they
reached Iskere, the last village before the Kutwal Valley. At Iskere there
were fields of wheat and maize, and as they moved on from the village
and joined the right-hand curve of the approach to the Kutwal Valley,
there was a profusion of colourful wild mountain flowers, and soon
they were passing through dense and beautiful pine woods. With their

first view of Haramosh round the next corner, it had been the most wonderful end to a journey.

In their journey across Pakistan they had been approaching Haramosh from the south-west. At Gilgit they had reached just about the same latitude as Haramosh, though they had still been some fifty miles to the west. From Gilgit they had travelled east-south-east to Sussi, and then trudged north-east in a long curve until, at the Kutwal Valley, they came out on the north side of Haramosh. They were starting their reconnaissance from the north because a survey of the southern approaches by the Italians in 1954 had indicated that there was no route from that side.

Despite the powerful impression of light and space in the Kutwal Valley, it was very little wider than the gorge they had recently left. The illusion came from the slanting white walls, the azure ceiling and the mosaic of the floor.

The Mani glacier filled almost the whole of the Kutwal Valley. But in its failure to fill the valley completely it had left a margin on the opposite side to Haramosh, a green and fertile margin which at first was only a few hundred yards wide, but which opened out towards the head of the valley where the hills on that side receded. The dividing line between the glacier and the fertile margin was marked by the lateral moraine, a long, low, knife-edge ridge squeezed up by the swollen glacier, with pine trees sprouting from the top, running down the valley like a rule.

It was where the fertile margin was at its narrowest that they pitched their first camp, because here they found a lake, the Kutwal Sar, and a spring of fresh water. Here, too, they were directly opposite the main summit. They might not be able to find any sort of route up the north face, but from here they were centrally placed for reconnoitring both the eastern and western approaches.

And as well as being the most suitable place to camp, surely this was the most beautiful spot in the whole valley. They were in the middle of an open area between the upper and lower clusters of the straggling village of Kutwal, with its primitive structures and inescapable smells. They could look higher up the valley to where the shepherds tended their sheep. They could see goats and even mountain ponies in the surrounding meadows and on the lower mountain slopes. These were the high pastures, where the people of the dusty gorge brought their animals for the summer grazing. Here they were right opposite that magnificent north face. They were far enough up the valley to get a good view of the complex of peaks that formed Haramosh II, and beyond it, right on the curve at the head of the valley, of the Haramosh La, the formidable pass leading out of the valley, the lowest point in the great circle of peaks but still a height of 17,000 feet, about 5,000 feet above the head of the valley. It was the only point leading out of the valley which had been climbed.

Here, too, was the lake, a turquoise jewel, reflecting the blue of the sky, set in an emerald-green hollow, and fringed with birch and pine trees. Here they were close to the lateral moraine, sloping steeply up to its pine-topped ridge, beyond which was the glacier, the slope itself loose and boulder-strewn, unkempt, but with a curious tidiness of its own, like a rubbish tip. It was an abrupt contrast to the fertile plain, like old snow piled high on the edge of a football pitch.

And there, beyond the lateral moraine, was the Mani glacier itself, thrusting its way straight down the valley under the north face of Haramosh, curving away in the distance towards the gorge. This was the mountain's excreta, slowly suppurating, patterned by the traffic of its own imperceptible movement, lined and grooved like a snow-covered road.

The glacier was fed by a myriad snow gullies from the mountain and from the region of the Haramosh La, and swollen by three great hanging glaciers on the north face, parallel and evenly spaced, which forced their way down into the Mani like tributaries, joining it turgidly at the foot of the mountain. Terraced craters on the floor of the glacier had formed where avalanches crashed like bombs into the valley, rippling the glacier surface like a stone thrown into a pond. And the whole glacier was covered by its own flotsam, ton upon ton of boulders and rubble that it had dragged off the mountain, making it harder to walk across than a rocky beach.

Here, the glacier seemed like a malignant growth on the mountain, bent on its ultimate destruction, clutching it with prehensile fingers from the sky. But farther down the valley, above Iskere, where the glacier ground to a halt in a monstrous slag-heap hundreds of feet high, they had understood its inexorable creative purpose. There, freed by the rise in temperature, it emerged quietly from its chrysalis of ice into a trickle of water, bursting at last into a cascading stream.

Jillott and Emery had seen all this, though for them everything was dominated by the mountain – their mountain. But Rae Culbert, the New Zealander, Botany and Forestry graduate, had a much bigger eye for country. He could feel the challenge of Haramosh, but he was absorbed too by the setting, the whole Karakoram range, its position in relation to the Himalaya and to other mountain ranges. Whereas the eye of an Englishman was just about big enough to take in a real mountain, Culbert sought to follow where passes lead, to travel and live amongst the ranges.

Among the four students he was by far the most mature. Yet he was still only twenty-five. When he left the New Zealand Forest Service to read Forestry at Oxford on a scholarship two years ago, he had still felt extremely young in spite of his considerable experience. But when he got to Oxford he found himself a more complete person than the average Englishman of his age. And the years in England had confirmed his maturity.

Culbert had come to Oxford with everything in his favour – deep affinity with his work, a Botany degree from Wellington University, a lifetime of wandering in the backwoods of the South Island, and three years' experience in forest survey with the New Zealand Forest Service; not in the office, but out in the bush, living hard, handling and supervising gangs of men, engaged in the highly skilled work of quantity surveying and general forest survey.

He had never been so disappointed with anything as with his first year at Oxford. The lectures had seemed elementary and even childish, delivered mostly by chaps who were half a century out of date. They just didn't work like that in the bush any more. And the rest of the students were streets behind him in knowledge of forestry and in general science, so that, with no exams that year, he just didn't need to do any work to keep up.

It was easy, and galling, to look back and see his mistake. His grouch anyway had been little more than the natural one of an outdoor man confined to a desk. He should have kept ahead and increased his lead by doing his own reading, instead of virtually standing still. It was hard to regret the good times he'd had, but he'd spent far too much time chasing round Europe with a rucksack on his back. In all his travels he'd spent his time increasing his working knowledge of the forests, but it was the textbook stuff that he was weak on. It had only been the knowledge that he was giving himself the chance to travel that had kept him at his studies even back home.

In the second year the work had been more interesting, and he had buckled down and done his fair share. The Himalayan trip had taken up a lot of his time, but this had been his only outside interest. He'd met Greta by then, of course, but he was slow to make advances with women and she had been no more than an acquaintance. She appealed to him a lot, but he had sworn to stick to forestry and the Himalaya this year. Meanwhile he had plodded on steadily, dismayed at times by the way the others had caught him up and even passed him on textbook forestry. Oh, it was the tortoise and the hare all right, neatly wrapped up.

Then, five weeks before his finals, he and Greta had somehow been thrown together, and that had been it. He'd never been so completely bowled over in his life. They'd both been sensible about it, trying not to see each other, but he had fallen hard for the first time and he just couldn't keep Greta out of his mind.

The exams had come and gone, and the third-class honours had come as a hell of a shock. Everyone who had done any real work had reckoned on getting a second. With the start he'd had two years ago, it seemed unforgivable to finish up with the also-rans.

It was not fair to say that it was anything to do with Greta. Those last weeks hadn't helped, but looking back he knew that he'd had it coming to him anyway. He'd got his degree, of course, and he knew the Forest Service would be satisfied. But he hadn't satisfied himself. If he'd worked hard on his books in his first year, he'd have kept ahead. But once he got behind on the textbook stuff he was in trouble.

It had been a bitter experience, a lesson he would never forget, but it had left him unembittered. Perhaps that was the chief thing.

Anyway, he must warn his brother about it. Bill would be arriving in the old country just about now to study at the Royal College of Art. He must urge Bill to get out in front and stay there. It was probably different with art: but the Culberts were sloggers, slow and steady and sure. They didn't come from behind.

And there was still Greta. That was the best thing that had happened to him in the old country. They weren't engaged or anything, just an understanding to wait a bit and see how things worked out, how they felt about each other after a few months' separation. They were both adult enough to do this without histrionics. After all, they had really only known each other for those last few weeks.

Culbert was a relaxed person. He could look forward to things without being impatient for them to come. It would be the same with going home. He hadn't been able to pass up this chance of climbing in the Himalaya, although it meant delaying his return home. Going back to New Zealand, seeing Dad and George, as he called his mother, was one of the most pleasurable things to look forward to; but this would probably be his one and only chance of seeing this magnificent country. Even after the climb, he thought he would probably latch on to a couple of the Hunzas and make his way over the Haramosh La, down the Chogo Lungma glacier, and then south to Skardu, before setting course for home.

He'd have himself sorted out by then. The disappointment over his degree would soften and he'd remember all he'd absorbed in the last two years. And he'd know whether his feeling for Greta was something he wanted to last right through life. He was pretty sure, for his own part, what the answer to that would be.

∞∞∞∞

At twenty-nine, Scott D. Hamilton Jnr was the oldest of the students. A graduate in Architecture and Political Science at Cornell, he was reading Philosophy, Politics and Economics at Brasenose. Apart from a short spell of National Service, he had spent the last ten years at universities. They were among the finest universities in the world, too; but to British eyes such an obsession for learning might seem to put him in danger of over-education.

Hamilton had many of those admirable qualities which are commonplace amongst Americans but which are not always to be found in Englishmen. He was frank and without artifice, ready to talk freely about himself, and always eager to please. He was an indefatigable organiser, revelled in publicity, and made one of the most significant contributions to the expedition by getting a £2,000 American press contract just when it was most needed.

He had felt at one point that his expedition colleagues were not properly appreciative of their good fortune in landing this contract. He had even wondered whether they might let it slip through their fingers, not so much through distrust of American publicity methods as through fear that the British rights might find their way to one of the less dignified English newspapers. The British were strange about publicity. In America, mountaineers had to write in order to climb: it was a natural hazard of their calling. Hamilton knew about the so-called characteristic British reserve, and of course some kinds of publicity were distasteful to almost everyone. But the British, and especially their mountaineering folk, were apt to pay lip service to the theme that all publicity was odious. They protested that they wanted to be left alone to their climbing; but they were quick enough to write books about it when they got back. Books, to the British, somehow lent a cloak of respectability to self-advertisement. A cover, if only a dust-cover.

Even so, Hamilton sympathised with the British attitude to sport, and preferred it to the traditional American attitude. He did not climb for the glory of reaching the summit, nor for the sake of the limelight. But he came from a nation which believed in self-advertisement, high-pressure salesmanship and the whole gamut of publicity. It paid off.

He believed, too, in progress, and climbing was another form of progress. Fields of exploration, like the German *Lebensraum*, had become overcrowded. Man had been forced to explore, as in New York he had been forced to build upward. The hundred years in which mountaineering had existed as a pursuit was the natural outcome of the discovery of the continents and the natural forerunner of space exploration. Once you'd climbed Everest, your thoughts inevitably turned themselves outwards.

But with it all, the magic of the unclimbed peaks remained, and Hamilton was a genuine wanderer and climber, loving physical effort and the open sky. Taller even than Jillott, he had trained hard for this expedition, was a teetotaller and non-smoker, did not gamble or swear, and was the very antithesis of the American playboy. His grandfather had emigrated from County Down, Ulster, his family strain was pure Scottish-Irish, and he had inherited their staunch Presbyterian faith. He was a Calvinist predestinarian, which he interpreted as meaning that he would exert his freedom of will as far as possible, and then abide by God's plan for his life.

His record in university activities showed him to be a meticulous organiser who quickly gained popularity in spite of his austere outlook. Bernard Jillott was the only person he had ever met who was a better organiser than he was, and as a result he had always held him just a little in awe. He knew how dedicated Jillott was to mountaineering, he came under the spell of his personality, and he envied the political know-how which made Jillott one of the best presidents of the OUMC in a decade. He admired Jillott's strong will, even though it sometimes led to errors of judgment, and felt that he understood all Jillott's good points and could sympathise with his weaknesses because they were his own. He was utterly devoted to Bernard Jillott.

Hamilton reserved his most unqualified admiration, though, for John Emery, whose versatile gifts and wide cultural tastes seemed to set him apart from the average climber. He could talk to Emery about his many other interests as he could not talk to Jillott, and when he needed advice on his various university activities it was to Emery that he went. But his ties with both men were close. He also felt an immediate affinity with Rae Culbert.

Hamilton's relationship with Tony Streather was of much shorter duration and was therefore not so well formed. There were a number of emotions in it. Two of them were certainly prejudiced – the admiration and respect he felt for Streather's achievements as a climber, and the slight but natural animosity he felt towards the famous mountaineer who had been called in to lead. Then, when he met Streather, he found him conformist, even colourless, almost synthetic. He didn't feel at ease with him. Perhaps his whole attitude towards Streather was governed by a bigger and deeper prejudice, a national prejudice – the traditional American idea of what a regular British Army officer must be.

Hamilton could never quite make out what Streather's motives were for climbing. He himself adhered to the romantic conception of mountain-eering, and the climbers he admired were Shipton, Tilman, Smythe and Geoffrey Winthrop Young. Hamilton was the only one of the party who consciously climbed for aesthetic purposes. He told his friends that he was going into the high places to think deep thoughts. It would not hurt him to go hungry for a while when millions in the world were starving, to take his turn at fighting for survival against the forces of nature. His puritan upbringing welcomed the hardship, the self-denial, the isolation. He felt himself to be a pilgrim, seeking after truth, privileged to breathe the pure mountain air and to see such scenes as expressed the power and the majesty and the glory of God. He saw nothing of humbug in any of this, and certainly not of hypocrisy. In his letters before leaving England he had quoted the 121st Psalm in full. Later, when passing through Karachi, he attended a church service at which this psalm was used as the text, and he was so deeply moved that he could not sit through it.

If Hamilton lacked anything, it was experience of the buffets of life, experience of the frustrations and conflicts with which the working middle class has to compromise. Thus he remained an idealist, sheltered by the high walls of learning, apt to take himself and life more seriously than most of his fellows. He had taken the extreme precaution of asking fellow students to be trustees of his property should anything happen to him, and had left written messages for his mother, girlfriend, chaplain and college with the Senior Dean of Brasenose before his departure. His preparations were so elaborate that when he said goodbye to his porter at Oxford the man burst into tears. But to Hamilton any other course of action would be irresponsible. Facing the dangers of the Himalaya, he was greatly concerned to put all his worldly affairs in order. For the rest, his New Testament would always be with him and would be read nightly.

To the rest of the party, much of this suggested a tendency to self-dramatisation. But generally they found him full of animation, disarmingly self-critical, and thoroughly human and likeable. He was a good climber, but not a mountaineer, and his place in the party was first in the preliminary organisation, and second as part of the survey team. In this he had the help of a Pakistani, Sahib Shah.

◇◇◇◇◇◇

Some people had mountains thrust upon them. Some even were thrust on top of mountains. So it had been with Tony Streather. He had joined the Indian Army at the age of eighteen in 1944, inspired by a school lecture. When partition came in 1947, he was serving on the Pakistan side of the line. He had already formed a deep affection for the country and its people, and he stayed there. It was in Pakistan that as a captain in the Chitral Scouts, familiar with the Chitral area and speaking the local dialects, he was asked by the Norwegians in 1950 to accompany them on an expedition to the 25,264-foot Tirich Mir as transport officer. In Chitral, transport meant porters.

It had been a successful expedition, and Streather had managed the local men with his usual unobtrusive efficiency. But far more than that, he had made himself so indispensable to the climbing party that he had stayed with them in the later stages of the climb and finished up with them at the summit, without any proper climbing equipment, clad for the most part in little more than a golfing jacket. When he came down, he found to his surprise that he had climbed higher than any other Englishman for fourteen years. And, more important to Streather, he had liked it.

Most Englishmen, he knew, began their acquaintanceship with mountains on a modest scale, graduating through Wales, Scotland, the Lakes or Derbyshire to the Alps. He had gone straight to the top of a major Himalayan peak. Soon afterwards, with the run-down of the British element of the Pakistan Army, he returned to England and joined the Gloucestershire Regiment. He found climbing in England and Wales a disappointment; after the Himalaya, the mountains lacked grandeur. In time he learnt to appreciate them and the demands they made on the climber. But his climbing experience had been like starting one's tobogganing career on the Cresta Run. Everything after that was in danger of being an anticlimax.

He found, again to his surprise, that he was something of a figure in the mountaineering world. He had climbed Tirich Mir. He didn't think he was a man particularly susceptible to flattery, but he had to admit that he had been warmed by the recognition he had gained, albeit fortuitously, as a mountaineer. Then in 1953 had come the American expedition to K2, the second highest mountain in the world. Two of the Americans had attempted to climb this mountain in 1938, and they knew the value of having a man who was familiar with the country, had the contacts, spoke the dialects and could take his place in the climbing party as well. They had heard of Streather from the account of the Tirich Mir expedition, and after consulting the Norwegians they invited him to go with them.

Streather had no false modesty. It was nice to be sought after. His knowledge of the language, locale and people, and his experience of man management as an Army officer, coupled with his physical fitness and quick acclimatisation, justified his place in any expedition of the sort. He had accepted, subject to getting leave from the Army. It had meant a considerable sacrifice at the time. The Army had given him four months' leave, unpaid, and he had forfeited the seniority as well. (He had got the seniority back later, but he hadn't known that then.)

K2 had established his reputation. Tirich Mir could have been a fluke – it probably was. But he had stood up to the tragedy on K2 better perhaps than most. And he had been climbing then with a group of men of such character and ability as might never again be assembled on a mountain.

He had kept going on K2 when most of the others had faltered. That might have been a fluke, too, because he was comparatively unhurt in the fall; but it had given him a firm and deep-seated self-confidence. Then in 1955 he had been one of four men to reach the top of 28,146-foot Kangchenjunga. His position in the forefront of Himalayan climbers was thus assured.

Streather was still in many ways a beginner as a climber, with little experience of Alpine or rock climbing, but he knew the Himalaya as well as almost anybody. Above 20,000 feet his stamina seemed to be sure. That, he knew, was his real strength as a climber: his quick and completed acclimatisation at high altitude.

Soon after returning from Kangchenjunga he got married, and this was his first expedition since then. Sue had been absolutely marvellous about it. Weekend after weekend she had endured the invasion of their home by the climbing party, as they packed, sorted and repacked, typed freight manifests, stencilled innumerable packing cases, arranged countless details, and talked and talked of nothing else but Haramosh. Towards the end their home at Camberley had looked more like a warehouse than an Army married quarter. Everything had been delivered there: all the food given by a multitude of commercial firms, running to hundreds of tins; all the climbing equipment, clothing, tents, ropes, sleeping bags, Primuses, medical stores. Sue had catered at various times for all the climbing party, sometimes all at once, put them up, and entered into everything with cheerful enthusiasm. And he wasn't only leaving Sue, either. He was leaving a four-month-old son.

Why did he do it? Well, there wasn't anything complicated about that. Climbing was fun. It was the kind of sport that appealed to him, because it was a hard sport, demanding absolute physical fitness. Not the fitness of the athlete – that was too brittle – but the fitness of the ascetic.

He was inclined to be scornful of romantic conceptions of mountaineering, particularly when these became emotional and extravagant, as he felt they often did. Mountaineering was a form of escapism; and as for perspective, if you couldn't think clearly in the valley, then you certainly wouldn't up there. Like the people who thought they drove better after a few drinks, the perspective idea was an illusion born of intoxication – the intoxication of height.

The years in Pakistan had given Streather something of that bigger eye for country which he recognised as being one of the things he had in common with Rae Culbert. He loved Pakistan, and this expedition was a wonderful excuse to get back there. He liked to move among mountains, was content to do so, and was not continually obsessed by their challenge. He needed very little from mountains but their company. But he had to admit that he enjoyed climbing them, perhaps because he had accidentally discovered that he was good at it.

Another thing he enjoyed was planning the climb. There was nothing esoteric about mountaineering. The difference between climbing a mountain and climbing a hump on the downs was only one of degree. You came to a bit of a sheer drop on one side, so you looked for a gentle slope on the other. Or if the ground was broken and rocky, you looked for a firm grassy ridge. Magnify the whole thing a hundredfold, cake it with snow and ice for weather and altitude, and you had the Himalaya.

He had come to look at hills as a tank corps man looks at rolling country, applying his specialised knowledge to every crink and curve. You made a survey of the problem, you decided on a plan of campaign, and then you tried it out. It was the ideal exercise for the military mind. Indeed it was no accident that the first ascent of the greatest of all mountains was planned and led by a soldier.

It was true that by the standards of his team he was uneducated, and compared with Scott Hamilton, he supposed, almost illiterate. Streather was two years older than Hamilton; but he was half a lifetime older in experience of life and people. There could hardly be a greater contrast. A captain at twenty-one, in sole charge of large numbers of men in remote districts of Pakistan, he had learnt complete self-reliance. His conventional education had suffered; but he had never found any difficulty in making sensible decisions and balanced judgments.

The most important thing after a few weeks in the Himalaya, confined to a two- or three-man tent in bad weather, under the strain of high altitude and a meagre diet, was compatibility. You had to fit in. Second came physical fitness, with climbing ability only third. All the big expeditions that he had been on had recognised this, and the climbing party had been chosen accordingly. But with smaller parties like this one, to lesser known peaks, the choice was more limited.

There would be some rough edges to be knocked off for all of them, in the next few weeks. That was inevitable. There wasn't a man in the world whose mannerisms you weren't capable of hating just a little after a time. Streather himself was used to the long days of waiting which beset every Himalayan climb, but none of the others were. He must try to see that everyone got what he wanted from the expedition. And he must make sure that none of them were allowed to take any unreasonable risk. Risks in mountaineering there must always be, but he was determined that nothing should happen to mar this expedition. No one knew the dangers better than he.

He hadn't quite admitted it to himself before but the truth was that, abundant as his pleasure was at being here, there had been a tiny element of duty about his decision to come. That might sound like a strange sense of values; but men who were fortunate enough to have experience of the Himalaya had a duty to pass that experience on.

He must keep clearly in all their minds that the initial aim was reconnaissance – to explore and survey the approaches to Haramosh. If the weather was kind, if all went well and they found a route to the top and they still had time to attempt it, well and good. They would gear their reconnaissance so that if a route opened up in front of them, they would have the resources to exploit their luck. They had set out in exactly the same way on Kangchenjunga, and four of them had reached the top.

Yet he had always felt that the chances of reaching the summit of Haramosh were slender. Time, the size of their party and the known ruggedness of the mountain were against them. And a sight of the mountain had very much strengthened this view. The north face was a freak; hardly anything elsewhere could compare with that sheer 13,000-foot drop to the valley. And they had already carried out a reconnaissance of the western approaches by two separate parties, which had shown that the mountain was unclimbable from that side.

Streather and Emery had climbed on the ridge which sloped up from the Mani glacier; Jillott and Culbert on the ridge immediately behind it, on the far side of another hanging glacier that swept down the mountain, out of sight from the valley. Both parties had reached about 17,000 feet fairly easily, but everywhere they looked beyond that, great pinnacles of rock barred the way, and the ridges became serrated or fell away sheer before rising almost vertically on the far side. Even if they could negotiate these huge buttresses, they would never get porters up there.

Jillott and Culbert had been able to look across to the south-western ridge, but this, too, was jagged and broken. They had ruled out the southern approaches before leaving England. Now, within a few days of being here, they had ruled out the north and the west. The only part of the mountain which they knew could be climbed was the La, and this must be their next endeavour.

Once established beyond the La, it looked as though they might swing round to the right along the snow-covered north-east ridge towards Haramosh II, and that this might eventually yield a route to the summit. But it was not a route that one would choose if any other prospect offered. It meant first climbing Haramosh II, nearly 22,000 feet high, descending perhaps 2,000 feet into the trough separating the two summits, putting probably three camps in that trough, and then finally attempting the ascent of the main summit.

And after this ascent, succeed or fail, they would have the long trudge back across the trough and then their second ascent of Haramosh II to accomplish before the real descent began. And they might well be delayed by weather between the two summits, which meant that at least one of the camps in the trough would need to be strong and well stocked. It was doubtful whether their small and modestly equipped party could establish such a camp in the time at their disposal.

But with all the obvious difficulties, it looked a feasible route. As far as they could see, it was the only feasible route; and each one of the climbers secretly held buoyant hopes of it. Even Tony Streather, conscious that he must be the steadying if not the restraining influence, felt the general wave of optimism. He had in his party skilful, determined and ambitious climbers, well suited, once the pyramid of camps was built, to a tenacious dash for the summit.

3

ABOVE THE HARAMOSH LA

In order to start the assault via the north-east ridge, they would need to move base camp up to the head of the valley, almost directly below the Haramosh La. But everyone was anxious to get on with the climb; so Streather sent Jillott and Hamilton ahead with two of the Hunza porters to establish a camp halfway up towards the La, while he and Emery moved base camp with the aid of local men from the village and the other four Hunza porters, and then went back to Sussi to collect the remainder of the stores. Hamilton had had what he termed a 'personality conflict' with the Pakistani surveyor, Sahib Shah, and Streather had decided to leave the surveying to the Pakistani and use Hamilton to help establish the lower camps. He was a good climber, and it would give him something worthwhile to do. Culbert was busy making a collection of flora in the valley.

The six Hunza porters had joined the party at Gilgit. They came from a people reputed to be descended from the invading armies of Alexander the Great, and held the same special place amongst expeditions to the Karakoram as the Sherpas held in the south-east. Three of them – Dhilap Shah, faithful servant of many expeditions; Rustam, a big, ponderous fellow; and the garrulous Shakoor Beg – were veterans in their mid-forties, in a country where old age came early. To Jillott they had seemed almost decrepit, and he had chosen two of the younger men, Nadil and Johar.

Nadil had a smattering of English and seemed a cut above the others, while Johar was the youngest and on his first expedition. Streather had already earmarked Nadir, the third of the younger men, as probably the best all-rounder, and he knew from experience that the older men, although they might be wrinkled and apparently in their dotage, would probably turn out to be the stronger carriers.

Jillott and Hamilton set off early next morning, carrying the food and equipment necessary to establish Camp I. Jillott's attention was fixed on the slopes up which they must soon make their way. The lower slopes were smooth and vegetated, spilling out into the valley like great plinths, and their route lay between two of these projections, across a wide snow gully or shoot, and up towards a snow buttress to the right of the La. Although at first the only snow was in the gullies, higher up it covered the mountainside except where the rock protruded through. They crossed the first snow gully as they would have done for the La route itself, then contoured round a grassy rib and made their way across another strip of snow. There was no sign of any recent fall, though some old avalanche debris formed a ridge down the centre. This brought them to another rib of grass which was pleasant to ascend. As they gained height, they looked back occasionally into the valley, now well beneath them. Suddenly Hamilton pointed to the snow gully they had just crossed.

'Look! See what we missed!'

A small avalanche was creeping down the couloir towards the place where they had crossed. It petered out just before it reached their tracks.

'I don't know whether to go on or not,' said Jillott.

'Well, we saw how slowly that one moved,' said Hamilton. 'If a bigger one came down, there'd still be time to run across.'

The Hunzas, however, had made up their minds. 'This place no good,' said Nadil.

Jillott decided that they ought to go on. They were leaving the danger zone behind, and above them the route didn't seem to be threatened at all.

Although at first uneasy, he soon forgot his fears. The route turned to loose rock and stones, not too steep, and he was going well. Soon they found a rivulet running down the mountainside, and they stopped to rest and drink. Nadil and Johar, who had lagged behind after the incident of the avalanche, caught them up.

'Johar not good,' said Nadil.

Johar sat down on a rock holding his head in his hands. Jillott estimated that they must be well above 13,000 feet; Johar was obviously feeling the effects of the altitude. As this was his first expedition, he'd probably never been as high as this before.

Jillott had a tube of aspirin tablets in his pack, and he gave two of these to Johar. Then he tried Johar's load. It seemed a lot heavier than Nadil's – a good forty pounds. Before he led off again, he exchanged his own rucksack for Johar's pack frame. As he swung the load on to his back, he almost regretted the gesture. But when he saw the gratitude in young Johar's eyes, and the mixture of surprise and approval in Nadil's smile, he was glad he had done it.

Now they were moving up a snow slope into which their deeply treaded climbing-boots bit crisply. Jillott kicked steps in the snow and for a time it was pleasant going. Then the forty-pound load began to tell, and he tired.

'I'll take over,' called Hamilton. Jillott kept on for another minute or two, but was then forced to give up, and Hamilton took over. Once the steps were kicked by the leader, it was easy going for those behind. Eventually Hamilton, too, tired, and Nadil called eagerly, 'Me, sir,' and showed that he had kicked steps before, although he moved slowly. At length, with Hamilton leading again, they reached an island of rock about halfway up the mountain flank at about 15,000 feet. There were snow gullies on either side, but the rib itself was clear of any threat of a snowfall. If they could somehow build a ledge out of loose rock, it would be the ideal spot for Camp I.

They set to work to build a terrace big enough for a tent. It was hard and unpleasant work, moving about on the steeply sloping scree, carrying pieces of rock; but when they finished, they had a level platform on which to pitch their tent. When the job was done, Nadil and Johar went back alone to the valley.

Here on the mountainside they could look across on a level with some of the lower precipices of the north face and appreciate even more fully its rugged defiance of the climber. But the trough linking the two peaks still looked feasible.

They spent that night at their new camp, their sleep disturbed by the noise of the avalanches thundering down the north face. In the middle of the night Hamilton called Jillott from the tent to take a look at one of these avalanches. Although falling almost sheer, it seemed to move slowly, and it was only from this that they got a true impression of distance and scale.

After breakfasting on porridge, Ryvita and marmalade, they left camp early next morning to climb up to the ridge, aiming for a point a little to the right of the La, but still virtually at the head of the valley. The first part of the route was over good hard snow, and their crampons bit nicely. But suddenly Hamilton shouted up to Jillott.

'Looks like one of my crampons has broken!'

'Oh, bad luck.' Jillott watched Hamilton sit down and try to adjust the troublesome crampon.

'It's broken all right. Guess I'll have to go back.'

It certainly wouldn't be safe on this stuff without crampons. And high above them, 1,000 feet below the ridge, Jillott could see a steep snow slope which they would have to climb to reach the ridge. He didn't mind cutting steps for Hamilton for a short distance, but up that last slope it would take far too long.

'You go on back, then. I'll keep going for a bit. See you back at Camp I.'

Within half an hour the snow thinned out and Jillott made his way on to a loose rock rib. It was hard going now, with the messy rubble underfoot sliding down underneath him so that for every two steps up he slipped back one. He could hear the displaced rubble skittering down the mountainside behind him. The ridge was rotten all the way, and he kept away from the right-hand edge, which dropped away 3,000 feet down the flank of the mountain.

At length the loose rock changed to a smooth snow rib and he put on his crampons again. Ahead of him, the snow rib led to a steep snow face, at the top of which was the ridge. Above the ridge was an incredibly blue sky. So far he had been in shadow, but the snow slope was glistening in the sun and he put on his snow goggles.

The slope was almost as steep as it had looked from below, fully fifty degrees, but his crampons were biting beautifully, and he began to feel a tremendous sense of freedom and elation. It was the first real climb of the trip. Soon he would be over the rim, and he was excited at the prospect of what he might see.

The slope eased, and he came out on to a wide snow col, a sort of plateau blunting the ridge. He walked on across the col and ahead of him he could see the snow surface falling away gently to the Haramosh glacier.

Here, 6,000 feet above the Mani, was this huge wide glacier, like a flyover railway, sweeping down from the heart of the Haramosh massif to join the Chogo Lungma glacier to the east, peeping over the La as it went by for a fleeting view of the Kutwal Valley below. Looking west, to his right, Jillott could see that the whole width of the glacier some distance above this point was broken by an icefall where the river of snow and ice changed its level. It looked impassable. And immediately to his right, the north-east ridge leading up towards the complex of peaks that formed Haramosh II was a fantastic switchback. They would probably have to find their way through the icefall first before searching for a route.

Jillott looked across the glacier to the high ridge on the far side, and then down towards the Chogo Lungma, where several 20,000-foot peaks were pushing up through banks of cumulous cloud. Then he turned back and retraced his steps across the plateau. This would make an ideal site for a good strong camp to support the assault on Haramosh II.

He allowed himself a long stare down into the Kutwal Valley from the crest of the ridge, and then set off down the snow slope. He was surprised at the steepness of the descent. Perhaps it would be too much for the porters. Anyway, it might help if he cut some steps now to prepare the route for them. It was far too steep for him to be able to reach down and cut steps as he descended, so he cramponed down a pace or two and then cut up. After an hour of this he had cut about a hundred steps, and he was beginning to tire. He kicked rough steps down the rest of the way, then walked as the slope eased. His crampons were balling now.

He reached the rib of loose rock. He couldn't help kicking lumps off at almost every step. The sun was on the back of his neck now and he began to feel hot. Below, he could see the long snow rib above the camp, and then the rock island itself, with Hamilton outside the tent, waving up to him. He half kicked and half slid across the snow rib down towards Hamilton, and collapsed at his feet. He had been climbing alone for nearly five hours.

The American was a good friend at these times. He fetched water and made coffee. They ate sardines and biscuits. Then they began the descent to base camp. Jillott, rested now and invigorated by the day's progress, glissaded excitedly down the snow gullies at the foot of the mountain and reached base camp half an hour ahead of Hamilton.

It rained heavily that evening and most of the next day. Hamilton and Jillott had left their brightly coloured windproof anoraks at Camp I, but nevertheless they set out the next morning, together with Rae Culbert and three Hunza porters, with loads for Camp I. They kept going throughout the morning and reached the rock island in three and a half hours. They built a second terrace some thirty feet below the first one, dumped their loads there and set off down.

Jillott was anxious to get Camp II established next day, so they spent the afternoon packing the next day's loads. Streather and Emery would be back from Sussi very soon, and he wanted to have some real progress to report to them. He was up early next morning, but to his annoyance the Hunzas showed no signs of life. A late start, and fresh snow on the mountain, forced him to change his plans. He decided to send Culbert and Hamilton, with three Hunzas and two porters from the village, up to Camp I with loads. Culbert and Hamilton would stay the night at Camp I and ferry the loads on to the Camp II site in the following two days. He himself would wait at base camp for the return of Streather and Emery. He hoped that in two days' time he and Streather would be able to go straight through to Camp II, on the plateau above the ridge, and then go on up the Haramosh glacier to establish a third camp beyond the icefall.

Meanwhile, Streather and Emery were on the last leg of the long trudge up from Sussi. They had walked the twenty-three miles to Sussi in a day, engaged thirty-seven porters, and then set out on the return journey next day. To Emery, Sussi had seemed sultry and unwholesome after the clean air of the Kutwal Valley, and the whole trip had been tedious and enervating. Streather, although suffering from a mild attack of dysentery at the outset, had taken the trip more in his stride. The two men had enjoyed each other's company, and the job had had to be done.

They quickly spotted each other's weaknesses and enjoyed a good deal of leg-pulling. Streather's dysentery had developed two days before they set out for Sussi, but it had been a long time before he would admit he was ill. Emery saw that here was a man who took great pride in his physical strength and for whom any form of illness was almost a character defect. The youthful and impressionable Emery, too, was an easy target for banter. They laughed at each other a lot, and this helped to make the trip more tolerable.

Already Emery felt complete confidence in Streather, both as a result of climbing with him on the western reconnaissance and from seeing the way he handled the loading at Sussi. He saw Streather as a man less obviously gregarious than himself, but sociable enough under the surface. Although superficially he had the characteristics of the regular Army officer, with all its strengths and limitations, beneath the regimental façade there lay a companionable, unprejudiced and by no means unimaginative character of great strength.

They arrived at base camp on the afternoon of 14 August to find Jillott awaiting them. 'I was afraid you wouldn't get back till tomorrow,' said Jillott. 'It's good to see you.'

'How have you been doing up here?'

'Not too badly, really.' They could tell from Jillott's obvious excitement that this was an understatement. 'Bit of a hold-up with the Hunzas this morning, but we've established Camp I and I've found a site beyond the La for Camp II. Culbert and Hamilton and two of the Hunzas should be up there tomorrow. They'll be at Camp I tonight.'

'Sounds as though you've done pretty well,' said Streather enthusiastically. 'We'll try and get up there tomorrow to have a look at what you've done. Then perhaps in two days' time you and I could go ahead and establish ourselves at Camp II.'

Next morning there was again no movement in the camp at six o'clock. Jillott emerged somewhat reluctantly from his tent and went across to get the Hunzas moving. Shakoor Beg and Nadil were supposed to be on duty. Tea was a long time appearing, and Jillott, keen to get on and show Streather the progress they had made, got more and more short-tempered. He decided to supervise the cooking of breakfast himself. He found the two Hunzas cooking chapattis. Surely they knew by now that the sahibs had porridge for breakfast. He threw the chapattis off the fire and put a pan of water on for the porridge. It seemed ages before the porridge was ready.

After breakfast Jillott sorted out the loads while Streather got up to date with the expedition mail. Twenty of the villagers turned up to act as porters, and Jillott packed up eighteen loads, the other two men taking firewood. It would save on paraffin.

The morning was well advanced when Jillott led the way up towards Camp I, hoping the porters would follow. Streather still had some letters to write, and Emery was treating some of his patients from the village, but they would catch him up later. Jillott tried hard to force the pace to make up for lost time, but every half hour the villagers sat down to rest, and as he had to keep them in sight he had to do the same. Their progress was thus only spasmodic, and they had only reached the grassy spur dividing the two snow gullies when Streather and Emery caught them up. He was anxious to hear Streather's opinion of the route.

'What do you think of it?'

'I think it's fine. Perfectly safe. And pretty direct. It's fine.'

He was relieved that Streather approved, and as they walked on together he felt far less strained. Emery began to forge ahead, but Streather and Jillott waited for the porters. They kept up their staccato progress fairly well until they came to the snow traverse below Camp I. Streather and Jillott led the way across. It was easy going – the slope was only about forty degrees, and good steps were already kicked – but only half the porters would follow.

'Let's go back and see if we can bring them over,' said Streather. 'It's probably just one old fellow who's scared, and he's talking them out of it. I'll see what I can do.' But he still couldn't persuade the porters to cross.

After a long discussion in Urdu, in which Streather got more and more annoyed, he turned back to Jillott and Emery.

'I've called them every name I can think of,' he said, 'and I've poured scorn on them, too. That usually works. I think some of them will follow us now.' But just at that moment a boulder loosened from above crashed down the slope right in front of the porters, and they drew back in alarm. All Streather's exhortations were wasted on them now. They flatly refused to cross.

Eventually, by carrying most of the loads themselves, and with the help of two of the less apprehensive porters, they got everything across to the rock island. Streather went down to pay off the porters, and Jillott and Emery stayed at Camp I.

Culbert and Hamilton returned to camp later that afternoon. They had had a frustrating time above Camp I and had failed to reach the ridge, being forced to dump their loads eventually when Johar, affected by the altitude, had collapsed with a headache. Hamilton had led most of the way; while Culbert held Rustam and Johar on the rope, moving one at a time on the snow slopes. Johar had never been on a rope before, and trying to tell him what to do, in a language he hardly understood, had been pretty trying. When Hamilton reached the last steep slope leading up to the ridge where Jillott had attempted to cut steps on the way down, he decided that it looked too steep and traversed across it to the right to gain a shallower rib. It was here that Johar had sat down with his head in his hands and refused to go on.

Jillott and Emery went down to the valley to help Streather with the next day's loads, and Culbert and Hamilton stayed at Camp I to try again for the ridge next day. They got away early, followed the easier route that Hamilton had chosen the previous day, dropped their loads above the La, and then went back for the loads they had dumped the day before. Then they ferried all the loads across the snow plateau to a possible site for Camp II.

This was the day that Streather and Jillott had planned to come straight through to Camp II, so that they could work up through the icefall next day. Culbert expected to see them soon after midday. They waited until early afternoon and then decided to start down. But when they reached the top of the snow slope the surface was shrinking and creaking unpleasantly. Neither Culbert nor Hamilton was sure what this meant, but the noise was frightening enough and they wondered if the slope was about to avalanche. They decided to await the arrival of Streather and Jillott.

By six o'clock that evening there was still no sign of anyone from below. The two men decided to stay at Camp II for the night and go down next morning, when the snow would be safer after the night's cold.

In fact, the carry up to Camp I had delayed Streather and Jillott, so that they did not reach the last stage up to the ridge until late afternoon. Here they followed Hamilton's route to the top. Both men were very worried at seeing no sign of Culbert and Hamilton.

Suddenly Jillott felt a crunching jerk from the snow he was walking on. He stopped instantly, as though his own weight and movement might touch off some deep disturbance of the snow.

'What was that?'

'The snow surface slipped a bit,' said Streather. 'But it's all right. It's really only a thin layer of ice stretched out over the snow that's making all the noise, and this slope isn't steep enough to avalanche, anyway.'

They went on. The snow still creaked beneath them alarmingly, but there was no sign of movement. Then, rounding a corner near the ridge, they saw Culbert and then Hamilton, Rustam and Johar. They had a tent pitched.

'Are you all OK?' asked Streather.

'We're all right,' said Culbert. 'We've been here since about half past ten this morning, but every time we tried to get down, the snow creaked as if it was going to give, and we daren't move.'

'It's just done that to us,' said Streather. 'But it's really perfectly safe.'

Hamilton turned to Jillott. 'We've been expecting you for hours, Bernard,' he complained. 'You said you were leaving base camp at six o'clock.'

'Yes,' said Jillott. 'I'm sorry. It took us a long time to get the porters going.' He turned to Streather. 'We'd better go down, hadn't we? There's only one tent. We can get back to Camp I if we go now.'

'Not a chance,' protested Culbert. 'We'll go down. We can follow your steps. Are they safe?'

'It's quite hard now,' said Streather. 'What about Rustam and Johar? Will they make it?'

'I reckon they'll be all right – they did pretty well on the way up.'

Hamilton, cold and tired and hungry, faced now with the prospect of scrambling down to Camp I in the half-dark, reiterated his complaint. 'We've been sitting here for hours waiting for you to come, Bernard.'

'We had quite a lot to do before we left this morning, Scott,' cut in Streather firmly. Hamilton recognised it as a mild rebuke. Even Jillott was taken aback for a moment at Streather's deliberate curtness. Hamilton admired Streather as a splendid man and a fine leader, but he began to suspect that beneath the polished façade there lurked a potential martinet. The man was a regular Army officer, and it couldn't be otherwise.

Culbert and Hamilton hurried off down with Rustam and Johar, while Streather and Jillott settled in at Camp II. They had only the green Meade tent, a two-man tent but a tight fit nevertheless, and they squeezed in and passed a tolerable night. Culbert and Hamilton followed the Hunzas down, but they lost them in the darkness, missed their way, and arrived an hour after the Hunzas – much to Rustam's and Johar's delight.

Next morning Streather and Jillott decided to wait for the sun to strike the tent before moving; but it rose behind a pyramid peak on the far side of the Haramosh glacier so that its rays were slow in flooding the plateau. They emerged from the tent at seven o'clock, cooked a good breakfast of porridge and sausages, followed by Ryvita and marmalade, and then began digging a hole for the stores that Culbert and Hamilton and the two Hunzas had brought up in the previous two days. Jillott was already feeling the altitude, and he noticed what an interminable time it took to accomplish anything. Lighting the Primus and cooking and eating breakfast took them nearly two hours. The tendency was to potter about and avoid serious exertion. Streather seemed much less affected and Jillott left most of the digging to him.

Together they scanned the north-east ridge leading directly up from the La over two subsidiary peaks to Haramosh II. It was obviously very broken, would be technically difficult, and would be totally unsuitable for porters. As Jillott had anticipated, they would have to move up through the Haramosh glacier and try to turn the flank of these subsidiary peaks beyond the icefall.

Meanwhile, at Camp I, Emery had been ready for an early start. He had been due to go up to Camp II with Hamilton, leaving Culbert to search for flora in the valley. But at five o'clock, when Emery stirred, Hamilton was still feeling the effects of the previous night, so Culbert decided to abandon his flora. 'I'm OK, John,' he said. 'Would you like me to come?'

'Very much.'

They took four Hunzas, with loads, and reached Camp II after three hours to find Streather and Jillott still there, just about to leave for the icefall. All four men were in good spirits and they discussed the progress they were making with great animation. Everything seemed to be going unbelievably well.

At length Culbert and Emery went on down to Camp I with the Hunzas, and Streather and Jillott plodded steadily across the Haramosh glacier to the far side. The icefall looked far less complex on that side. Then they began to ascend steeply into the icefall, and they roped up. Streather led the way, kicking steps up a soft and sugary snow slope of about fifty degrees. Jillott watched him intently. It was illuminating to see an experienced Himalayan climber at work. He noticed that Streather moved slowly, almost laboriously, but smoothly and with great effect.

'You've got to go slowly,' said Streather, reading Jillott's mind. 'And if you start panting, go slower still.'

When they reached the steepest and softest part of the slope, Streather stopped and called back to Jillott, 'Better take a belay, Bernard.' Jillott thrust the shaft of his ice axe deep into the hard-packed snow and wound the rope round it securely, while Streather moved on alone. Above the rise they were able to move together again. They crossed some old avalanche debris which had come down from the ice cliffs on their left, and then they were in the icefall itself. Here they were in a world of fantasy, a Walt Disney landscape in which odd and grotesque shapes and sizes stared down at them or opened their jaws to swallow them whole. These were the glacier's rapids, forming a monstrous sloping tank-trap, a petrified cascade of ice and snow. It was a cubist's nightmare – nature overwhelming the modernists at their own game.

They zigzagged back and forth as in a maze, seeking the way round crevasses, avoiding overhanging ice blocks which might choose this moment to fall on them, keeping the rope almost taut, moving one at a time, dragging their ice axes in firmly to take the strain of a fall. The crevasses were mostly at right angles to the flow of the glacier, so that as the level changed the lower lip of each crevasse was several feet below the upper, like an enormous open cut. All too often there was no link between one level and the next, so that they were forced further and further to the left. Occasionally they were able to make progress by crawling across snow bridges, accumulations of snow resting on strips of glutinous ice that clung to both sides of the crevasses and thus formed a bridge. Some of the crevasses were so wide, and the change of level so great, that Streather thought they would never get porters and stores across without a horizontally placed ladder. But at last after crawling on their bellies across a precariously lodged snow bridge over the widest and deepest crevasse of all, one at a time and firmly belayed, they came out into an upper snow basin above the icefall.

Now the glacier sloped gently on into the distance, bordered on either side by a high ridge. Their problem would be to find a way up from the right-hand side of the glacier towards Haramosh II.

'This looks like our route all right,' said Jillott.

Streather nodded slowly. Their route would come through here.

'We may as well go back now,' he said.

Back at Camp II, they made ready for an early start next day, filling two flasks of coffee and getting into their sleeping bags in the Meade tent as soon as the sun went down. Jillott, however, couldn't sleep. The excitement of the day was still upon him – it had been their most successful day so far – and he was troubled by the altitude, feeling nausea almost continually and suffering an attack of fast, deep breathing during the night, which was so bad that Streather alongside him couldn't sleep either. Streather got up and opened the flap of the tent to give Jillott more air, and after that Jillott dozed a little.

Streather was about early, but the business of lighting the Primus, melting snow for their porridge, getting their boots on and clearing up the camp took them so long that it was nearly seven o'clock before they got away. Jillott was still suffering from anoxia, but he drank his flask of coffee and took three aspirins and felt a little better.

They crossed the glacier basin in shadow but the peaks on either side were glinting in the morning sun. The condition of the snow was ideal, and they cramponed easily up towards the slope leading to the icefall. The sun hit them at the top of the slope as they crossed the old avalanche debris. They stopped and put on glacier cream and snow goggles, and took off their anoraks and dropped them just short of the icefall.

The track they had made the day before was still good, and within an hour they reached the point where they had turned back last evening, just above the icefall. Contrasting with the extreme cold in which they had set out, it was now really hot, the sun beating down on them from a clear blue sky. The heat was having its effect on the snow, which was softening rapidly, making the going difficult. Streather led the way, circling to the right above the upper snow basin to avoid a steep face of ice cliffs that threatened to discharge their excess snow down on to the glacier on the left. At ten o'clock they stopped for breakfast. Jillott had recovered sufficiently to enjoy sharing a tin of pilchards, and they drank water from their water bottles and chewed snow. The sun was scorching.

The going was so heavy now that there was little point in trying to push further ahead. They dumped the stores they had brought with them beyond a slight rise above the upper snow basin, at a point which looked a likely site for Camp III. All the visible slopes up towards Haramosh II were broken or threatened by ice cliffs, but further up the glacier they could see a snow slope on the right where they could probably avoid any threat of avalanche. This led up to what appeared to be a snow plateau. A reconnaissance would be necessary, but here was a possible site for a camp from which the final assault on Haramosh II could be mounted.

The sky clouded over in the afternoon, and by the time they got back to Camp II the air was getting chill, but the heat of the day was still reflected in the angry sunburn which had afflicted the fair-skinned Jillott. His neck, lips and nose were especially painful. He took a sleeping pill, and this gave him a good night's rest.

Next day Streather and Jillott carried forty-pound loads up to the point above the icefall where they had thought of siting Camp III. The old snow had settled down nicely and their crampons bit with a satisfying crunch. On the way they straightened up the route, fixed marker flags in the icefall, and put a fixed rope on the final snow bridge that they had crawled across the previous day. They decided to move the projected site for Camp III about a hundred yards forward, well above the snow basin and on the gentle upward slope of the glacier. They ferried the first day's loads up to this point as well, and marked the dump with flags.

Now they had a fine view of the snow slope leading up towards the shoulder of Haramosh II. It was concave – fairly gentle to begin with, then steepening rapidly in its later stages, like a retroussé nose. Once established at the top of that slope, they would be within striking distance of their first objective.

When they got back to Camp II they found that Culbert and Emery had moved up with a four-man Whymper tent and were prepared to stay. Hamilton had also been up and had led the Hunzas back to Camp I. The camp immediately above the La – Camp II – was now a formidable one, well stocked and fully able to support the ascent of Haramosh II. They discussed their plans for the next few days excitedly.

'Everything's going splendidly,' admitted Streather. 'All we want now at Camp III is a tent and a couple of sleeping bags. Tomorrow four of us will go up to Camp III with loads, and John and I will stay up there and try to force the route to Camp IV. Meanwhile, over the next two days Scott will move up here with four Hunzas to strengthen this camp, which now becomes virtually our base, abandoning Camp I. Bernard and Rae, with the help of the remaining Hunzas, will fix the ladders in the icefall. Then you'll be able to get the porters to bring heavy loads through to Camp III.

'Once we've established Camp IV, I shall make way for you, Rae. Then you and John can try straight away for the summit of Haramosh II.

'I'm going steady with you, Bernard. I want to get you fully acclimatised before I push you too hard.'

Jillott acquiesced in this. Streather's summary had been no more than a recapitulation of an animated discussion by the whole high-altitude team. And Jillott was content to let the others have a go at Haramosh II. It was only a stepping-stone, and his turn would come.

They spent the remainder of the afternoon packing the stores for the next day's carry up to Camp III. They dug a better pit for the stores that were to be left at Camp II, wrote a few letters, and started to cook supper. Then the cloud that had been building up during the day began to descend on them, and a patter of hail tore at the canvas tents to announce the coming storm. Soon it came thicker and faster, snow and hail together, beating noisily on the tent roofs. They hurried inside, leaving Culbert to finish the cooking alone. When he brought the meal into the Whymper tent, he was covered in snow.

'The weather's been good so far,' said Jillott. 'Let's hope this doesn't last long.'

'We're well ahead of schedule, though,' said Culbert. 'We can stand a day or two of crook weather.'

It was still only 19 August. They had arrived in the Kutwal Valley only a fortnight ago. Haramosh II was almost in the bag. And they still had nearly four weeks' climbing ahead of them.

They had got so accustomed to good weather that they hadn't thought much about its turning bad. Yet Streather had warned them repeatedly that when bad weather set in it might keep them confined to their tents for days on end.

'I don't want to depress you chaps,' said Streather, 'but this stuff looks like settling in. We're in for about three days of it, I'd say.'

Jillott moved in with Culbert and Emery in the spacious Whymper, leaving Streather, who had earned the privilege by winning the toss, in solitary comfort in the Meade. But before they went to sleep, they were drawn from their tents by a desire to gaze once more at the twin peaks which they now had such high hopes of conquering. It was a moment that none of them would forget.

The first flurry of the storm had subsided, but the wind was still rising, and it was snowing steadily now. The valley was a pool of near-darkness, but visibility to the north was still good, and the distant peaks were bathed in a curious, yellowish light. Horizontal blankets of cumulus lay at different heights in a layer-cake of cloud. Above them a ceiling of high wispy cirrus was building up, and the sky, which earlier had looked incredibly close, was now as remote as it had seemed from the valley. There was the usual chill in the air for late evening, but it was a damp rather than a brisk chill, a subtle change that Streather alone of the climbers could feel. But the atmosphere deeply impressed them all. It was an oppressive, menacing, bilious world. For all the progress they had made, the main summit of Haramosh still looked incredibly distant, arrogant and inviolable. No one spoke his thoughts. They crawled back into their tents in awed silence.

4

TROUBLE WITH THE HUNZAS

For the next forty-eight hours it snowed unceasingly, so that any movement other than digging out their tents, cooking meals and answering the calls of nature was out of the question. Most of the time they stayed in their sleeping bags, reading. After the exertions of the last fortnight, the lull was not altogether unwelcome. Jillott particularly was grateful for the chance to recover from the effects of the shrivelling sun. His lips, swollen and blistered, were very painful.

At least another foot of fresh snow fell during the second night, burying the food and Primus stove that they had left outside the tent. Streather's small Meade tent was almost completely smothered. Most of the time he hibernated, read *War and Peace*, and emerged only to poke his head in the entrance to the Whymper to see how the others were faring. 'All this deep snow is very bad,' he told them. 'It'll be several days before we can push ahead again. We really ought to go down in order to conserve our food stocks here, but I'm afraid the snow slope between here and Camp I won't be safe.'

Culbert was reading *Elephant Bill*; Emery was deep in Stendhal. Emery was finding acclimatisation in a sleeping bag at 17,000 feet a surprisingly satisfying experience. The demands of companionship, environment and self were refreshingly simple. One read, wrote a little, ate occasionally, and the hours passed from dark to light and then to dark again, without any sense of the passing of time. One didn't have to bother about washing or changing, very little movement was required, and one was sufficient in one's sleeping bag, with Stendhal for the mind and chocolate for the stomach. It was the most soothing of anaesthetics, a dichotomy of thought and action. Culbert, too, was relaxed and quiescent, a model of passivity. Jillott's sunburn was better, and another day would certainly help, but he would have been quite pleased to move on. To a young man of his volatile nature, inactivity was always irksome. And he was beginning to miss his food.

In search of a square meal, he emerged from the tent into the unfriendly white world. A few breaks were appearing in the clouds, the light was dazzlingly bright, and it was snowing gently. He dragged the tarpaulin cover off the food dump and found a tin of meat, some curry powder, and a tin of soup. He wanted something for a sweet, perhaps treacle pudding. It must be over on the far side of the dump. He heaved again at the tarpaulin, which was laden with snow and difficult to move. He groped underneath the edge, but he still couldn't find what he wanted. He reached for a shovel and dug feverishly at the piled snow. At this height such violent effort soon had its reaction, and he sweated and panted. He moved the tarpaulin a fraction, and a cardboard box lay revealed. Jam, not treacle pudding. He tugged the box to one side and it disintegrated, spilling tins of jam in all directions. That was the end. He flung the tarpaulin back over the hole and stumped back to the tent with what he had.

If mountaineering involved this sort of unpleasantness, then give him climbing every time. He got far more enjoyment from a climb in the Cambrian mountains in the warm sun of a Welsh afternoon than from load-packing over easy glaciers and roughing it in a tent. In future he would sit out stormy weather in front of a blazing fire in a mountain pub.

Damn the ethics of greater mountaineering! He would content himself, and indeed be more than content, with a rock problem in Llanberis.

The effort was more concentrated, the satisfaction of achievement more immediate. He began to wonder whether he would be back home in time for the Welsh dinner at Llanberis on 6 October. Suddenly it seemed irresistibly desirable. He was homesick for the mountains he knew and loved; he was homesick altogether. But even as nostalgia overwhelmed him he knew that, however much he might long for the comforts of home – a hot bath, ham and eggs and honest bread to eat with it, and a spacious desk to write at – when he got them again he would yearn with equal longing to be back here on Haramosh, cold and hungry and in the middle of a storm.

He got out of his sleeping bag and cooked the dinner, and felt better for having done something positive. Afterwards, as the evening drew on, the sky cleared a little, and it seemed that they might be able to get down to the valley tomorrow. The prospect of a good meal at base camp cheered him a lot.

That night, crawling out of their tents of necessity before finally settling in, they looked out on the same yellow world of two nights ago. There were the same horizontal grey clouds, lined with the same sickly light, an eerie, ochreous phosphorescence. Rakaposhi alone, fifty miles distant to the west, etched its silhouette in bold blackness. They shovelled snow away from their tents, talked in hushed tones, and crept quietly back into their cosy, predictable world.

It snowed again in the night, but eventually petered out into a grey dawn. The bad weather showed no sign of abating, but Streather decided that the lull was sufficient for them to get down to base camp. He had to arrange their return bookings, reorganise the porters, and attend to several other business matters. And there was the paramount consideration that they must conserve their food stocks at Camp II.

Emery, who suffered very much from the inertia of starting – once he got going he was all right, but getting underway was a tedious operation for him – greatly disliked the idea of abandoning his position at Camp II.

He was snug in his tent; and any move downwards seemed a retrograde step. When the weather cleared, which might be tomorrow, they would only have to come all the way up again.

'Couldn't Bernard and I stay here?' he suggested. 'Then we could make the best use of the first fine weather, instead of wasting a day struggling back up here.'

Jillott, too, found himself ready to invent reasons to justify his inclination, though his own purpose happened to be opposite to Emery's. He wanted to go down.

'I agree with Tony,' he said. He was sorry to leave Emery arguing alone, but the thought of roast lamb at base camp overcame comradeship. 'We ought to go down.'

Streather shot a questioning glance at Emery, but could see that the more he was opposed the less likely he would be to move. He decided to let him have his own way.

'You can stay here if you like, John,' he said, 'but the rest of us must go down. Don't forget that you might be stuck here on your own for several days if this weather goes on. You can't come down alone.'

Emery refused to be convinced, and Streather let him stay. Obstinacy was a quality which was part of the makeup of every mountaineer; inevitably it got misdirected sometimes. It was better for Emery to learn the lesson his own way. There was plenty of food at Camp II; one person wouldn't seriously reduce it, and he would be perfectly safe provided he stayed put.

'If the weather's any good at all I'll come up again tomorrow,' compromised Jillott.

They roped up and Jillott led down. The fresh snow made the journey more difficult, and they took five hours to reach the valley against the normal three and a half. Passing through Camp I, they found Hamilton with two of the porters, leading the life almost of a recluse, eating little more than biscuits, and lying in his sleeping bag writing poetry, but evidently quite content. 'If it's still snowing tomorrow,' said Streather, 'you'd better come down.'

Emery, alone at Camp II, spent the morning digging out the pit of stores. A great deal of snow had drifted under the tarpaulin, and he spent several hours clearing it. He was rather looking forward to a day or two's hermitage, and he spent the rest of the day happily, cooking and reading.

He passed a somewhat restless night, and awoke early to find it snowing again. He turned over and went back to sleep. By eight o'clock, when he finally got up and went outside the tent, the snow had stopped, but he was dismayed at what he saw. The entire sky was filled with high black storm-cloud, and the atmosphere was still and becalmed. Earth and sky seemed motionless, waiting and watching, under a smooth metallic canopy. It was quite unlike anything he had seen before, but he felt certain that it presaged a further spell of prolonged bad weather.

He began to regret his reluctance to move yesterday. The hermitage that had been so pleasant to contemplate now filled him with misgiving. His natural gregariousness returned with a rush. He wanted very much to be with the others.

A day or two by himself had seemed attractive, but four or five days, perhaps a week or even more, would be intolerable. He could just see the tracks of the others disappearing over the ridge. If he was going he must go now. Another fall of snow and the tracks would be obliterated.

In spite of what Streather had said, he felt confident of his ability to get down. There was no time to bother about breakfast. He ate a bar of chocolate, tidied up the camp, fastened everything down, fitted his crampons and set off across the col. As he followed the tracks down the steep slope of the mountain, it began to snow steadily. He hadn't been a moment too soon.

The only part of the route that gave him any real difficulty was the traverse between the two snow ribs above Camp I. Here he had to cut new steps at first, and it took some time. But he reached Camp I in about two hours. He shouted as he approached the tents, but did not expect an answer, and he was astonished to find Hamilton still there, completely on his own. He was perfectly happy, had sent the two Hunzas down, and was quite prepared to stay where he was.

'Come down with me, Scott,' urged Emery. 'You can't stick up here alone much longer. It's bad for you.'

But Hamilton refused to move, and Emery, having overcome the first inertia, was anxious now to keep going. On the way down to the valley he passed two of the Hunzas carrying a note from Streather to Hamilton. It read, 'Come down and get some decent food in you. Either you're not getting enough to eat up there or you're using up the kerosene.' No doubt Hamilton would follow him down.

Nearing base camp, Emery began to anticipate his welcome. They would be pleased to see him, but he had more or less come down against orders. Yet he had climbed by himself before, and being able to see the tracks had been the decisive factor. It was one of those things that it was difficult to justify except to oneself. If anything went wrong, then of course everybody said you'd been a fool.

He had to face a good deal of banter when he got to base camp. Streather said he ought to be court-martialled, and suggested Dhilap Shah as president of the court.

'Why Dhilap Shah?'

'Because I happened to overhear a remark he made in Urdu to the other Hunzas when you arrived.'

'What was it?'

'Well, freely translated, I should say something like "the silly bugger, coming down alone".'

Hamilton arrived a few minutes later. Much as he enjoyed solitude, it had been high time he came down. It was now 23 August, three weeks after they had left Gilgit, and the whole party was back at base camp.

That evening they tuned in as usual to the weather forecast that Radio

Pakistan broadcast for them after the news. 'Here is the special forecast for the Oxford University Haramosh Expedition,' intoned the announcer in impeccable English. These forecasts, besides being extremely useful to them, gave them a comforting sense of contact with the outside world.

'Cloudy at 12,000 to 14,000 feet,' the voice said. 'Wind from 180 degrees at 15 knots. Temperature 24 degrees.'

Cloudy – that was an improvement, anyway. And next morning to their surprise the sun was shining and the weather looked much better. There were banks of cloud still drifting up the valley, but Streather decided that it ought to be possible to make a carry through to Camp II. Culbert had some collecting to do on the way up to Camp I, and he himself was anxious to attend to a few business matters and sort out the details of the return trip, since if the weather held they would be going up to stay. So he sent Jillott, Emery and Hamilton, together with all six Hunza porters, the plan being for the three climbers and two of the porters to go lightly loaded straight through to Camp II and stay there, and for the other four Hunzas to travel empty to Camp I, pick up loads there and take them up to Camp II, and return to base that night. If the weather still held, Jillott's party would go on to Camp III tomorrow and Streather and Culbert would follow them up. The big push to Haramosh II would begin.

They began their preparations early, but they took the usual interminable time to get started. Jillott, who was particularly keen to get going again, fretted impotently at the delay, while Emery and Hamilton, thoroughly disgruntled at having to go up the mountain again after having come down only the night before, stumped about moodily. They eventually got away at nine o'clock, Jillott leading, Hamilton and the Hunzas following, and Emery, still not ready, setting out a few minutes later. Jillott pushed ahead, but Nadir and Johar chose a more direct route up the first snow ridge and Jillott was unable to keep abreast of them. When he reached the first scree section he found them resting on the boulders. He sat down beside them.

'Better route?' he asked.

The youthful Johar beamed with delight. 'Yes, Sahib. Up.' And he gesticulated to indicate the greater directness of the route they had taken. Jillott gave them some chocolate and a swig of his lemonade flask. Hamilton and the other Hunzas arrived, and Shakoor Beg wheedled some more lemonade out of Jillott, which the Hunzas shared. Then they went on.

The snowfield immediately below Camp I was in very bad condition, and several small snowslides swept down the couloirs and overflowed on either side of the rock island which supported Camp I. Hamilton was caught in one of these slides and very sensibly thrust his ice axe in where he stood and stayed put. The snow soon petered out and he came to no harm.

The idea had been to evacuate Camp I altogether, taking everything up to Camp II. But when they reached the rock island Jillott was appalled to see how much stuff was still there. He began to dish out the loads. When he had given everyone what he judged to be a fair weight, there were still numerous odd items strewn about. He gave some kerosene and part of a pressure cooker to Rustam. Rustam objected, but he took no notice. To Johar's load he added a Primus stove and the rest of the pressure cooker. Johar looked at him mutely but appealingly. He added several miscellaneous pieces to Shakoor Beg's load, and before he could protest, took two or three of them off again. Shakoor looked pleased – the Sahib was trying to be fair! It was a trick to remember. Nadil got a sack of food – mostly grapefruit juice. Nadir got Hamilton's personal kit and another Primus. Dhilap Shah got a mixed bag of food. Ten loads remained. He gave Culbert a note to take back to Streather telling him about these loads.

Emery and Culbert discussed the weather, which was beginning to look threatening. The clouds were rolling thickly up to the head of the valley, gradually gaining height, rising up towards them. Jillott saw them too, but decided to ignore them. They had been at Camp I too long and he was getting impatient at the delay. He sent Hamilton on with the

Hunzas while he and Emery tidied up Camp I and swallowed a few hasty bites of food.

The porters were heavily laden, and they moved very slowly across the first piece of snow up to the rock rib. Occasional small snowslides were coming down here as well. One wiped out the steps of Hamilton and the porters as Jillott and Emery prepared to cross. But they soon caught up with Hamilton, and Jillott and Emery took over the lead and began to force the pace.

It was getting late, about half past one, and Jillott was beginning to wonder whether the four Hunzas who were to return to base would be able to carry their loads as far as Camp II. But he was determined that they should, and, with Emery ahead of him making the track, he pressed ruthlessly on.

The cloud from the valley had pushed its way up above the mountain and now lay oppressively above their heads. As they reached the end of the rock rib it began to snow heavily. The day which had promised so well had turned sour on them.

They reached the final snow slope leading up to the col above the ridge. Jillott put his crampons on quickly and hurried on past Emery. This was the crucial point. If he could keep them going now, they would make it.

He glanced back over his shoulder and saw Emery stop to put on his crampons, then his anorak. Hamilton followed suit. He could see that the porters didn't like it. They huddled together and glanced up at him once or twice. Shakoor Beg as usual seemed to be doing most of the talking. He waited for them to follow.

Emery was calling up to him. 'They've put down their loads and they're going back.'

Jillott's patience cracked. He had to get those porters moving again somehow.

He raced down the snow slope towards the astonished porters at breakneck speed, did a full somersault to pull himself up, and arrived unceremoniously at their feet. He was too upset to consider what might be the best way to coax them to go on, and he found himself shouting at the top of his voice.

'You're going to Camp II!' He tried to make it a statement, but it turned into a threat. 'Pick up those loads and get going. Do you understand? Get going!'

They muttered amongst themselves and regarded him doubtfully. 'Down, Sahib,' insisted Nadil. 'We go down. Snow not good.'

'Get up there,' Jillott screamed back at him, pointing up the slope. 'You don't go down till you've done your job.'

Shakoor Beg and Nadir began another animated conversation, and then Shakoor turned to him and spoke vehemently in Urdu. Jillott was so enraged by this that he raised his ice axe as if to strike him, and Shakoor cowered down, expecting the blow. Jillott restrained himself with difficulty.

Again the Hunzas burst into a babble of Urdu. Only Dhilap Shah, the faithful veteran, remained aloof, the only one still shouldering his load. If only he could rally the others round Dhilap Shah. Johar, too, looked guiltily at him, but he was young and would follow the others. Jillott stood watching them helplessly, seeing them suddenly as people, not mere load carriers, his anger spent.

'Up for one hour more, then down,' he said. It was the last hope.

But the Hunzas ignored his appeal. Dhilap Shah still stood erect, but the others made as if to go down. Jillott turned to Emery in mute appeal.

Emery had watched the scene with mixed feelings. He understood Jillott's frustration, but his sympathies lay with the Hunzas. It was obviously going to take longer than usual to reach Camp II, and four of the Hunzas then had to return to the valley. They certainly wouldn't make it before dark. He would have sent them back straight away. But he felt he must offer Jillott some support. He turned to Nadir and repeated Jillott's last plea.

'Up for one hour, then down.'

'No, Sahib. We go to Camp II tomorrow. Now, we go down.'

Emery tried another tack. 'If Dhilap will come up with us, will you come with him?' Dhilap Shah and Nadir were the two who were supposed to stay at Camp II.

Nadir looked undecided for the first time. He talked to the other Hunzas for a moment, and then turned back to Emery.

'Yes, Sahib, I will come.'

The remaining Hunzas quickly stacked their loads on a ledge and set off down. Jillott led off up the slope, kicking the steps viciously, forging ahead with fierce energy, taking it out on the snow. The others followed.

'We'll just have to dump our loads at Camp II and come back for the rest of the stuff this evening,' he told Emery and Hamilton. They said nothing. It would be all they could do to get to Camp II before dark. They would have to fetch the other loads the next day. Jillott would calm down soon, and then he would realise how impossible the idea was.

Jillott didn't stop until he reached the col, and by this time his anger had cooled. They would ruin their chances of doing anything tomorrow if they flogged themselves too much tonight. In the morning, if the weather was bad, they could go back to the ledge for the other loads. If the weather was good, they would be better employed pushing on to Camp III. The Hunzas would bring the loads up eventually.

He sat down in the snow on the col with Emery and Hamilton. Nadir and Dhilap Shah were not far behind. When they arrived, Jillott jumped up and thanked them, shaking them both warmly by the hand. Both men looked gratified. Dhilap Shah's eyes were smiling kindly in his wrinkled face. He said something in Urdu, and Jillott could only guess at the meaning, but he knew the old man was with him.

Camp II was wet and cold, the tents full of food and personal kit. Little by little they sorted the big tent out. Reaction was setting in for Jillott.

He felt sick and dizzy, and his stomach was upset. Emery and Hamilton cooked the supper.

When they crawled into their sleeping bags it was snowing hard. Jillott took some sleeping pills, but his altitude sickness persisted and he slept only in snatches. If only all the Hunzas were like Dhilap Shah! He had supposed that a show of anger might lash them into action, but he had been wrong to lose his temper. He had felt Emery's unspoken disapproval keenly. It had been a miserable day.

Next morning they went down to the ledge to pick up the four loads left by the Hunzas. Nadir and Dhilap Shah took a load each and Jillott, Emery and Hamilton shared out the other two loads. The snow was deeper and softer than ever, and visibility was poor. They all moved very slowly. When they reached the col on the way back to Camp II, the mist thickened so badly that they had to wait several minutes until it cleared sufficiently for them to get a glimpse of the route. Eventually they dumped the loads at Camp II and set off down to base camp. The weather was obviously turning bad again. Jillott raced ahead of the others, glissading wildly down the soft snow below Camp I. Once, running into a patch of dirty ice that looked like scree, his feet shot away from under him and he slid some sixty feet, bruising and scraping himself and giving himself a nasty fright. But when he picked himself up he found he wasn't seriously hurt, and he continued to rush down.

Streather greeted him as he walked into base camp. 'We thought it would be too bad up there for you today.'

'It was pretty unpleasant,' admitted Jillott, 'but by no means impossible. We got the four loads up that those blasted porters dumped yesterday.'

'Good.'

'I think they should lose a day's pay for refusing to go on,' said Jillott.

'Come,' said Streather, 'it would have been silly of them to have gone any farther, wouldn't it? They weren't down here till eight o'clock as it was.'

'Eight o'clock?' echoed Jillott in astonishment. 'What were they doing until that time? They left us at ten to four. They should have been back before seven.'

It looked as though the Hunzas had loitered on the way down to make good their story. Anyway, it was obvious that Streather thought Jillott had been wrong to try to push the porters further. He felt crushed and hurt at this lack of support.

There was more depressing news at supper. During their absence, Streather and Culbert had worked out a plan of attack. 'Once the weather clears up,' Streather told them, 'we need twelve days to get to the top. But to do it we shall have to tighten our belts. We simply can't take a lot of food to the high camps.'

Jillott felt for the moment that he would have preferred to eat rather than get to the top, but he was too fed up to argue. He ate his supper in silence, smoked incessantly afterwards, and crawled into his sleeping bag that night in complete dejection.

5

THE LOST FOOD DUMP

Next day, 26 August, the weather was particularly bad, and it remained so for another three days. The party was concentrated at base camp, with morale becoming progressively lower as time passed. Interest mostly centred around Streather's assault plan, which still held out a remote hope of success. Based as it was on limiting the amount of stores they carried to the higher camps and keeping the margin of surplus food as narrow as safety permitted, it gave them, if the weather should ease, a sporting chance of reaching the top. Every mouthful was accounted for, so that, if they got to Haramosh II or near it, and found there was a possible route on, they wouldn't be beaten for the sake of a couple of days' food.

When they had planned this expedition in the first place, they had realised that they were not coming to the Karakoram at the most favourable time. The best time was probably May and June, after the winter snow and before the summer rains; but it had been a question of fitting in with the end of term at Oxford and the summer break at Sandhurst. The problem here was very different from the region around Everest, where the climbing season was governed by the monsoon.

The monsoon came up across the Bay of Bengal and unleashed its ferocity on the Calcutta area and the south-eastern Himalaya around

Everest and Kangchenjunga. Once the monsoon broke, climbing in this area was finished for the season. But the monsoon dissipated its strength as it crossed the continent, so that by the time it reached Lahore and Rawalpindi it began to peter out. In the Karakoram, you didn't get a true monsoon. It spilled over into the area just a little, but August and early September, which were virtually impossible in the south-east, were generally fairly good up here. The weather was perhaps less predictable in August, alternating between periods of three or four days' good and bad weather, but by September it generally settled down into a long fine spell.

Thus they had been content to do their reconnaissance, look around, find a route, and then hope for two good weeks in September in which to go for the route they chose. But the last two weeks had been so bad that they were still a long way from Haramosh II, and much of the work they'd already done above Camp II would be negatived by fresh snow. In addition, the pattern of the weather was strangely unfamiliar. Instead of August beginning badly and improving as it gave way to September (Streather remembered this well on K2), it had begun beautifully but then deteriorated and got worse and worse as September approached.

The chances of getting to the top were slim, but it was still possible with a long spell of fine weather. Much would depend on what they found above Camp III. When they had carried the stores up to the proposed site for this camp, Streather and Jillott had seen a slope which looked as though it might take them to a camp site from which they could mount the assault on Haramosh II. This perhaps would be the real climax to the trip, the end of the second act. Once on or near the top of Haramosh II, they would know whether the trough between the summits could be crossed.

Streather had in mind that, in spite of the need for a strong camp in the trough in case the weather broke, a camp just this side of Haramosh II might be no further from the main summit than the last camp from which Hermann Buhl had reached the top of Nanga Parbat. It was pure speculation, of course, and Streather had no intention of letting anyone attempt such a lone marathon unless all the conditions favoured it; but he could not and would not ignore the fact that Jillott was very much of the Buhl temperament. There was nothing Jillott would revel in more than a long, desperate rush for the top.

Streather had no illusions about the strength of his party, and he had no illusions about its members. Irritating as he sometimes found Jillott's habit of seeming to think of nothing but his stomach, he recognised that food was the essential fuel to a man who expended his physical and nervous energy in the prodigal way Jillott did. After a hard climb, or a brush with the porters, he had to recharge his batteries. He recognised, too, that Jillott had qualities and abilities as a climber which, perhaps above the rest of them, marked him out for greatness. Here was a man who would be quite prepared to burn himself out in one glorious endeavour. His singleness of purpose would see him through, and he wouldn't count the cost. While he was still on the way up, his goal before him, he wouldn't give a thought to getting down. Emery, too, was potentially a great climber, in sheer climbing ability certainly Jillott's equal. These two men were the tanks, capable of busting their way through. He and Rae Culbert were the infantry.

Meanwhile, Jillott himself was slowly becoming reconciled to his position and adopting a more philosophic attitude. It wasn't strictly his show any longer; he was still making many of the detailed decisions, which Streather was content to confirm and ratify, but the major decisions were bound to be Streather's. He recognised that this was inevitable, and in any case, whatever he felt about it, it was his own arrangement and he couldn't alter it now. The final assault couldn't last much more than a fortnight, and he would do everything that was required of him and get the most he could out of it. He had got over his annoyance with Streather for not supporting him in his quarrel with the porters, and he had discussed the assault plan with him amicably enough. But he still felt that Streather attached far too little importance to food. It seemed that, to Streather, anyone who gave his stomach any thought at all was a glutton.

There had been an incident during the three days' wait at base camp which had illustrated the difference in the two men's attitude to food, and which had also illustrated how this and other such differences were falling into perspective. High cloud had spread up from the west in the morning, an umbrella of cloud had grown around Haramosh and low raincloud had billowed up the valley. Serious climbing had been called off, but Jillott had packed loads for himself and three of the porters to try to get some extra stores through to Camp I. It was true that the loads had been mostly food, including such comparative delicacies as marmalade and fruit salad, but it had seemed to him to be worth doing. It might well have given them something in hand later. Just as he was setting out the rain started, and in the same moment Streather and Emery returned from the village. 'All you want to do, Bernard,' Streather had chided him good-naturedly, 'is to get your bloody marmalade up the mountain.' Emery had cut in with, 'Bernard, you look like a small boy who's been caught doing something wrong.' Jillott had no doubt that that was exactly how he did look, but he was capable of enjoying a joke against himself, and he had joined in the general laughter.

Emery found life at base camp less disagreeable than he expected. He needed action almost as much as Jillott, but once action was suspended he accepted it with more resignation. For him, it was a time for reflection and anticipation. Paddington still seemed a long way off, and he was beginning to find that he could pick up the threads of his friendships before the boat trip, and even contemplate the voyage itself without pain. Medical treatment for the villagers of Kutwal, too, gave him something to do. One youngish-looking fellow complained of impotence. There could be half a dozen reasons, but he gave him a box of pills, enough to last him six days, and hoped for the best. The fellow returned the following evening, looking distinctly pleased with himself. He had taken all the pills in one go. And what was the result? Streather translated the reply carefully. 'He says he's much, much better – especially at mealtimes!' They did not enquire further.

The delay presented no problems to Streather or Culbert. Streather was used to it; Culbert spent his time collecting plants in the valley. This was another facet to Culbert's character – his complete absorption in a rare mountain flower, the meticulous way in which he kept and annotated his botanical collection. Hamilton, too, had other resources to fall back on. He was an enthusiastic recorder of detail, and he was for ever scribbling away in his diary, making what he called his 'notations'. It was wonderful what he found to write about.

On the evening of 28 August the forecast was bad, but it was a cold, clear, starry night, which normally meant good weather. As the sun went down, Emery wandered over to the stream that ran past base camp. The clouds had parted a little and their borders were etched clearly with crimson flame. Such a moment surely could not last. But then the dark curtains rolled back still further, and though the brilliance faded, a deeper, stronger light filled the valley as the stars appeared in the calm night sky. He plunged his face in the icy, chattering water of the stream, and gasped, almost shouting with the shock. He felt the hills large and strong about him, and suddenly he knew that whatever the future might hold, nothing in life would ever really break him. He had an overwhelming sense of freedom and impregnability, a vision, a revelation of eternity. The gift of life had been given and it would always go on.

The morning was clear, but they mistrusted it, waiting for the usual cloud to float up the valley and envelop the mountain. But by eleven o'clock the cloud was still only scattered and intermittent, and Streather decided that this should be D-Day, the first in his twelve-day assault plan. He, Emery and Hamilton set off with Nadir and Rustam to go straight through to Camp II. Jillott and Culbert and the remaining Hunzas were to follow them to Camp I, taking heavy loads on to Camp II next day.

The going above Camp I was very heavy, the whole route now being snow-covered where previously rock had protruded through. Their old tracks were no longer visible and the route had to be remade, so that they didn't reach the col till after dark. Camp II was in a disorderly state, and both tents were half buried in snow. Jillott and Emery had left this camp four days earlier in the middle of a snowstorm, and it had been impossible to clean the site up properly. The snow since then had turned disorder into chaos. But their first thought was to get the next day's weather forecast. Emery had laboured under the weight of the radio all the way up from the valley, and he set it down gratefully in the big tent and they tuned in hurriedly.

The forecast followed the seven forty-five news bulletin. They sat huddled round the radio in the semi-darkness, intent and motionless. Someone lit a candle and its flickering light pointed their features in shadowy relief and made their frost-encrusted beards and eyebrows glisten. They were still breathing hard from the effort of the climb and of clearing the tent and assembling the radio, and their moist breath filled the tent with steam. Even down in the valley the voice from the plastic box had been oddly comforting; up here at Camp II it was a voice from another world, a voice from the plains, reminding them almost chokingly of the friends in all parts of the world who were wishing them well.

The forecast was fair – as good a forecast as they had ever had. They were all tired from the hard climb, but the prospect of good weather fortified them. The tents were wet and unpleasant and they threw everything out and dug the fresh snow away. There was just enough light reflected from the snow for them to see what they were doing. The main task of clearing the site could wait until the following day; but even so, it was eleven o'clock before they turned in.

Normally the pattern of life at the higher camps was to get to bed about six thirty, relax and sleep, and be about early next day. But after the late night they lay in next morning; and then began the serious work of clearing the site. They had to dig for all the stores – snow shovels, flags, fuel bottles, Primus stoves, pots. They shovelled the snow off the tarpaulin covering the food dump, and then cleared the food dump itself. They piled the snow up around them, and when they finished they had dug the whole area out so completely that the camp was now sited in a pit.

Jillott arrived from Camp I soon after midday. He had been able to crampon all the way now that the route was snow-covered and the track had been made, and he was thoroughly enjoying himself. As he approached Camp II, he looked for signs that Streather's party had been able to press on towards Camp III. But the snow across the glacier was trackless, and there were no steps up into the icefall. This was a disappointment. It looked as though they had decided not to move today. As he got nearer he saw first Nadil, then Streather. He hailed them. 'Is the snow too soft to go on today?'

'It took us five hours to get up here yesterday,' said Streather, 'and then we found the camp in a ghastly mess. We've spent all this time clearing it up.' Jillott realised that he and Emery had left the place in a muddle, and he thought for a moment that Streather was blaming him. But then he was handed a flask of tea that had been specially saved for him, and he realised that Streather was doing no more than explain why his party was still in camp.

'Where's Rae?' asked Emery.

'Bringing up the rear,' said Jillott. 'He's got a bad throat and he's not going well. I think I'll go back and see how he's doing.'

He met Rae struggling up to the far side of the col.

'Let's have your load,' he called out.

But Culbert wouldn't have it. 'She's right,' he said.

Jillott brought him down with a rugby tackle, and Culbert then handed over his load. During his period of depression, when he had been feeling somewhat resentful towards Streather and Emery, Jillott had developed a strong affection for the New Zealander.

Streather, Emery and Hamilton got away at three o'clock to remake the track into and through the icefall. Once they had trodden the fresh snow down, it would be easier to move up to Camp III the next day. Up the long, steep slope into the icefall the going was appalling, and they sank into the soft snow up to their chests with each step. To make progress they had to lean forward into the snow, beat it down a little with their arms and elbows, then knee it down still further, and finally tread it in. They got about halfway through the icefall, as far as the first marker flag, which was just showing, but there was no time to attempt to get through to the dump of stores which would become Camp III.

They were away for over two hours. Camp II looked impressive when they got back; there were now five tents pitched, and all five climbers were there, together with four of the porters. The other two were at Camp I. Next day they would all make a carry through the icefall and finally establish the site of Camp III.

Streather and Emery were up at six o'clock, and Jillott poked his head out of his tent half an hour later. Streather was ready to go, but Emery was still sorting himself out. 'I don't think we need to rope up on this first bit,' said Streather. 'You'll be ages yet. I'll go on and improve the track and wait for you at the icefall.' Emery started out twenty minutes later, and the two men remade the track through the rest of the icefall. Many of the crevasses were bridged by fresh snow, and the most difficult part was the big crevasse near the end, which had widened considerably since the last time they crossed it. Here, Emery took a belay and Streather advanced to the lower lip of the crevasse, leaned out across the gap, and cut a step in the high crevasse wall directly opposite. He then swung the pick of his ice axe into the wall above him, and used this as a leverage to get a foothold on the step. Meanwhile Emery paid out just sufficient rope, taking up the slack when necessary. His end of the rope was wound round the shaft of his embedded ice axe, and he was standing on safe ground.

The upper lip of the crevasse was ten feet higher than the lower, but although it was steep it was not vertical, so that Streather was able to cut steps for himself to the top while Emery continued to pay out the rope. Once at the top, Streather in turn moved on to safe ground, took a belay with his ice axe, and then took in the rope tautly while Emery followed in his steps. The whole tricky operation was managed neatly and without fuss in a matter of minutes.

Once beyond this crevasse they were virtually through the icefall. But there was no sign of the marker flag or the ski sticks which Streather and Jillott had left sticking out of the snow at this point twelve days ago. The marker flag didn't matter, but the ski sticks were a loss as they would have been useful in the snow basin or col leading up to Camp III. It was a sobering reminder of the volume of snow that had fallen since they were last here.

'This means the stores you and Bernard dumped at the site for Camp III will be buried, too,' said Emery.

'We know where we left them,' said Streather. 'We'll probably have to dig for them, but they'll still be there.'

◇◇◇◇◇◇◇

Meanwhile, at Camp II, Jillott was getting the Hunzas moving and organising the day's loads. By having only tea and Ryvita for breakfast, and giving the Hunzas the same, he managed to get away at nine thirty. Hamilton came with him, but Culbert, although much better, decided after persuasion by Jillott that another day in camp would be good for him. They made good time in the steps of the others up to the icefall, where they stopped to rope up. Dhilap Shah had a ladder and the Meade tent. Rustam had two ladders, Nadir and Johar a kitbag each of food. Jillott took Nadir and Johar, and Hamilton the two with ladders.

Jillott kept well ahead of Hamilton's rope. The icefall seemed to have changed a lot, and only one solitary flag still showed above the snow.

The tracks followed a different route. They did not go over the first snow bridge, but over another part of the crevasse that had filled up with snow. One of the ladders had been intended for this point, but the new snow bridge looked secure and Jillott decided to take the ladder on. It might come in handy later. He stopped before the last crevasse. It had opened up a lot, part of the bridge had gone, and the ice tower that formed the near lip of the crevasse looked very unstable. He ran his eye up the steep upper lip, following the steps cut by Streather. It must have been an interesting crossing.

He wanted to use the cine camera, so he waited for Hamilton, and then sent him across the crevasse first, belayed by Rustam, filming him the while. Hamilton made it look impressively difficult. Dhilap Shah and Rustam followed. Jillott went next himself, leaving Nadir and Johar below. Now they fixed the ladders together and bolted them. Then Hamilton, belayed by Rustam, and with Jillott still operating the cine camera, lowered the ladder into position across the crevasse and tied it with rope to aluminium stakes. On the lower lip, Nadir and Johar dug and stamped the ladder into place. Then Nadir crossed the ladder, belayed by Johar, and last of all came Johar, belayed from above by Nadir. Now, with the ladders gone, they redistributed the loads.

They caught Streather and Emery up in the upper snow basin, and Jillott, lightly loaded, went on ahead to make the track. After about half an hour he began to think he must be near the dump of stores. He remembered that there had been a definite ridge running right across the basin, which they had followed a bit to the right with the idea of siting Camp III behind it. But ahead of him all he could see was a blank whiteness. The sky was obscured by pale cloud, and the lack of direct sunlight and shadow made it more than usually difficult to detect any slight rise and fall in the snow surface.

'I don't think we can have passed it yet,' said Jillott. They were all getting tired now, and they sat down to rest.

'Let's leave the packs here and wander around for a bit,' suggested Jillott. The others agreed. 'I'll go on up a bit to look at the next rise,' he went on. 'I'm sure we haven't reached the spot yet.'

Jillott ploughed on up the slope. The snow was still soft and thick and it was slow moving. It would be a serious loss to them if they failed to find these stores, as already they had cut their supplies down to a minimum. But he still felt confident of finding them. They had marked them with flags and stakes, and although the snow had covered them they couldn't be far below the surface. When he came to the spot, he would recognise it. He saw Streather move off to the right to follow the line of a slight upthrust there. Only three of the six porters were following.

Suddenly Jillott knew he was right. He had reached a much more definite ridge in the snow than anything they had passed previously. He shouted down to Streather, and began scratching about with his ice axe for some sign of the dump.

Streather called up to him. 'We'll pitch the tent down here and then have a look round later.'

'Send the porters up here then, will you? They can help me dig for the stores.'

'I'm afraid they're in a pretty Bolshie mood. They won't move.'

'Tell them they won't get any cigarettes if they don't come and help,' retorted Jillott. He was ready to get pretty Bolshie himself. 'I don't think I can find the dump by myself, but four or five of us together could cover the ground systematically.'

'They're sitting on their backsides and they've dropped their loads,' said Streather. 'They certainly won't come any further.'

Jillott bit his lip in anger, but went on scratching with his ice axe, and said nothing. Streather seemed to take anything from these porters. Did they have to give in to them every time? He gave up scratching by himself and rejoined the others.

'You didn't give them anything to eat this morning,' said Streather.

So they had been telling tales. 'They had the same as we had,' protested Jillott. 'A packet of Ryvita and a jar of jam. If I'd left them to their cooking we should have been there all day.'

'They say they're hungry and their feet are cold,' said Streather.

'Of course they're cold,' said Jillott. 'So would I be if I sat in the snow doing nothing.' He simply couldn't understand the passive, philosophic attitude adopted by Streather. The porters were paid to do a job, and if necessary they ought to be driven to do it.

Streather began to try to explain it to him. 'These men don't eat like we do normally, you know, Bernard,' he said. 'They've got no stamina to fall back on. Just look at them. Their belts are tightened already.'

Jillott saw the force of this, but he always seemed to be falling out with Streather over these porters. He didn't believe in all this kid-glove handling. He regretted losing his temper that day on the way up to Camp II, but he had finally got two of the porters to come up with him. He stood by despondently, watching Streather and Emery pitch their tent.

'These men are like children,' continued Streather. 'They quickly get dispirited when they're cold or tired or hungry, and they just give in. They haven't the reserves that we have, physically or mentally. Leave them to sit about for a quarter of an hour and they come round with their tails trailing.'

'Hmm,' said Jillott doubtfully. He guessed Streather was right, but he was far too impulsive to handle people like that.

Streather talked again to the porters. He seemed to be bringing them round. 'They're still worried about their feet,' he told Jillott. 'We'll rustle up what spare canvas overboots we can for them. Dhilap Shah and Rustam say they'll come up here again with loads tomorrow and the next day. Altogether they've done jolly well today. It's quite a business for them getting through the icefall.'

'I think I can find one or two more spare pairs at Camp II,' said Jillott. 'Perhaps I'll manage to get all four of them up again.' He began to feel more optimistic. Altogether it had been a highly successful day, and much of his keenness and enthusiasm was returning. He would be bringing them up here for the next two days, and by then Streather and Emery would have established Camp IV and would be within reach of Haramosh II. Already he was looking ahead. 'Do you think it's any use trying to persuade two of them to stay up here the night after tomorrow to help us make a carry to Camp IV?'

Streather looked dubious. 'I don't know. They're not really equipped for it, but it might speed things up. It depends entirely on how they're feeling at that particular moment. If it's a fine day, and you start out in sunshine, I should think it'd be worth trying.'

Streather realised that any faults that Jillott might have were purely the result of his abundant energy and enthusiasm, and he felt that he had got across to Jillott something of his own sympathy for the Hunzas. These two men were beginning to understand each other.

'We'd better be off now,' said Jillott. 'I hope you find the dump tonight.'

'So do we. We've got no Primus or kerosene until we do.'

Jillott joined the Hunzas, and they started down. Johar looked up at him sheepishly. 'Oh, Johar,' said Jillott, shaking his head reprovingly. Johar followed closely in his footsteps, and looking back a few minutes later he saw that the young Hunza was getting behind and was having a great struggle not to cry. He waited for him to catch up. 'It's all right, Johar,' he said kindly. 'Here, have a glucose tablet.' Johar brightened at once and his eyes were full of gratitude. They went on together.

At the ladder he roped each man down in turn, following them across after coiling up the rope. Then they wound their way through the icefall. They were following the morning's tracks and he didn't think there was much danger, but he went ahead himself just in case.

Down the steep slope into the lower snow basin he raced on ahead, reaching Camp II half an hour ahead of Hamilton and the Hunzas. He was very happy to find Culbert up and about.

'How's the throat?'

'She's right!'

Culbert had cooked an admirable supper – soup, curried mince, potatoes, cabbage, treacle pudding and stewed apple. Everything was just right and it all appeared promptly and without fuss. The weather forecast that evening was 'fair to partially cloudy', which sounded reasonable. Jillott went to his sleeping bag in a much happier mood.

Meanwhile, at Camp III, Streather and Emery spent two hours digging for the dump of stores. Eventually it began to snow and they were forced to retire to the tent. Unable to cook anything, and, even more important, unable to melt snow down for liquid, they ate a cheerless meal of biscuits, sardines and snow, moistened at the end by a tin of fruit salad each. Streather had a bottle of water three-quarters full, but he decided to save this for emergencies. They would be in an unpleasant spot if they couldn't find the dump the next day and the weather closed in.

While they were digging they had a good view of the concave snow slope leading up towards the possible site for Camp IV. Everything depended now on the condition the snow was in. What they wanted was hot, sunny days to pack the snow down followed by cold nights to freeze the surface hard. But all the time they were digging, black clouds were building up round the complex of peaks that formed Haramosh II, and round all the neighbouring peaks. It was a nasty evening. If it was a bad day tomorrow, and if they still couldn't find the dump of stores, it would just about kill any chance they had of getting to Haramosh I.

The lack of liquid would be particularly weakening now they were reaching a higher altitude. Normally, at lower altitudes, the air was moist and one breathed it easily. But as one climbed above 10,000 feet the air became progressively drier, so dry that it could not be sucked into the lungs without the addition of moisture. This moisture came from the body, and as you breathed the air out again, you exhaled the moisture with it. Thus you needed a very large liquid intake or your body became desiccated. This was no problem while you had plenty of snow and a Primus and kerosene. But without some means of melting the snow, their bodies would quickly deteriorate.

It started snowing again early next morning and showed no signs of letting up. The tracks they had made the day before with such time and effort had just about disappeared. Fresh snow was blowing and drifting into the steps, and it was obviously very doubtful if the party from Camp II would manage to get through that day. If they couldn't find the dump, they would have to try and get down, and this might be very difficult if it continued to snow.

In the afternoon the snow stopped and they began to dig at once for the stores. They could find no trace of anything. The sun shone briefly, melting some of the snow on their tent, and they mashed this up in their cups with lemonade crystals. It wasn't really liquid, but they spooned it up and chewed it until it melted completely. It was a cold mixture, and they sat in their sleeping bags to eat it so as to conserve body heat, which they could almost feel evaporating as they ate. They couldn't go on like this. It was infuriating not to be able to find the food and stores they had brought up before the weather broke, but the next day if the others didn't come up they would have to go down.

For Emery it was one of those days that belonged to the lost world where time stood still. It was like a day spent ill in bed, when dusk came upon one without one having realised that the day really existed. He recorded his impressions in his diary. The hours had accumulated softly and effortlessly, like snow settling quietly on the ground. Like snow they were ephemeral and lacked a separate expression, even in the memory, where they passed quietly into that limbo of half-images which dreams inhabited. He was pleased with what he wrote.

As a result of the lack of water and hot food, they were both feeling weaker the next day. The weather cleared a little, and the sun melted the snow on the tent roof. They mixed it again with the lemonade crystals, but it was a nauseating mixture. They decided not to do any more digging, but to conserve their strength for the effort to get down to Camp II.

They waited about for some sign of Jillott's party, but no one appeared. Then they went some way down towards the icefall, remaking the track, clearing away the deep new snow, and hoping all the time to see the others ascending. There was still no sign of them, so they stumbled back to Camp III, packed a minimum of gear, and set off wearily down. It was about midday, the icefall would be treacherous, and the whole track was smothered in snow. If the party from below didn't come up to meet them, they would be many hours getting down.

The previous day, at Camp II, Jillott, Culbert and Hamilton had been about early, knowing that if they were to get up to Camp III and back again they must leave camp by about eleven. But it went on snowing, and they gave up the idea of moving. It brightened a little about midday to worry their consciences, but it was too late to start then. And in fact it snowed intermittently throughout the day and the cloud never lifted from the upper snow basin.

Hamilton announced that he liked cooking. Culbert winked broadly at Jillott – so far Hamilton had shown no great keenness in this line. But he insisted. 'I can make an excellent chocolate cake. And that's one thing you look for in a girl – to see if her cake goes down in the middle.'

Culbert summed up the reaction to this characteristically. 'Much bloody good making chocolate cakes here.'

'I'm going to make the supper tonight,' announced Hamilton. 'We'll have fishcakes.' He opened a tin and added water. The fishcake mixture swelled up immediately. Culbert tasted it and approved. 'Let's have three, in case the others come in.' Hamilton kept telling them how wonderful the fishcakes were going to be, and on the strength of this they decided to forgo the cod steaks they had put by and give them to the porters. Jillott cooked these in the tent. Hamilton went out to light the other Primuses. He planned to cook onion soup, carrots, the fishcakes and a treacle pudding. He got two of the Primuses going, but the third defied him and he brought it in to Jillott to fix. The pump had gone wrong and Jillott couldn't find a spare washer. By this time the soup was ready. They sat down in the tent and ate this together. Now there was a delay. Then Hamilton appeared with the carrots. 'Are these ready?' Clearly they weren't – they were almost raw. He brought the carrots back twenty minutes later, and the fishcakes with them. The fishcakes were extremely good, but because of the broken Primus the pudding never materialised. Even so, Hamilton had gone some way towards proving his point, and Jillott and Culbert had enjoyed being waited on.

Next morning it was fine and clear at Camp II, though there was still some cloud around Haramosh II and in the upper snow basin below Camp III. They packed the loads and got the porters organised, but it was after ten before they got away. Jillott led off across the glacier and up the gentle slope of the snow basin. The fresh snow was two feet deep, slowing them down to a crawl, and their heavy loads made every movement hard work. Culbert took over the lead at the bottom of the steep slope up into the icefall. The snow here was waist-deep and he could make no progress at all. He took off his pack and forced his way through in bulldozer fashion. The sun came out for a moment and in the strong light he saw the outline of their old tracks for the first time. He tried to keep to these, as here the snow two feet below the surface was firm.

Bit by bit, going back every now and then to retrieve their rucksacks, they made headway. It took them a further hour to get from the beginning of the icefall to the ladder. Here it began to snow. Looking back down towards the Chogo Lungma they could see sunlight penetrating the cloud, but ahead of them in the upper snow basin the cloud was piling up and visibility was bad.

It was in a rare break in the mist and cloud that Streather and Emery, peering down on their way from Camp III, caught their first glimpse of six minute figures, insects crawling along a white tablecloth. It was a strangely impressive sight, extending as it did over several minutes, as the two groups fought their way through the snow and closed the distance between them.

Streather and Emery were especially pleased to see Rae Culbert at the head of the advancing column, looking thoroughly recovered. He grinned up towards them, white teeth flashing out of a scrubby black beard, his whole body laden with snow. As soon as he was within earshot he hailed them with a typical crack: 'Didn't you bastards know better than to come out in this?'

After much discussion, it was decided that Jillott and Culbert should go on to Camp III with their loads, which included a Primus each and some kerosene, while Streather and Emery went back to Camp II to recover their strength, returning to Camp III the following day. It was impossible for the porters to get much farther and still get back to Camp II, so they went on a little higher, dumped their loads, and then Hamilton led them down. Jillott and Culbert would pick up these loads the following day, and also look for the lost food dump.

Streather and Emery continued on their way down to Camp II, slowly and shakily, but sustained by the thought of water, hot soup and hot stew at the end of the route. Streather enjoyed this meal as much as any he could remember, and Emery ate in gargantuan fashion and luxuriated in the sensation of a full belly.

Next morning, Streather wrote a series of letters with the object of putting their departure off to the last possible moment. They had previously arranged that he and Emery, who had to be back before the others, should be picked up by Jeep at Sussi on 16 September, and the remainder of the party two days later. Now he asked for the first Jeep to be ready for them at Sussi on the 19th, and three more Jeeps and trailers to be ready on the 20th for the rest of the party and the baggage. Even so, they would have to be back at base camp by the 17th, and they might have to allow themselves several days to get down, depending on what progress they made. It was now 3 September. At the most they had about ten days' climbing ahead of them.

Jillott and Culbert would probably be breaking fresh ground above Camp III that day or the next day, but the weather had been so cruel that they would almost certainly have to lower their sights in the next few days. Only a minor miracle could give them much chance of getting beyond Haramosh II, and even that might be beyond them. But Streather's last-minute alteration of the travelling dates, which would still just meet their air bookings, gave his team all possible chance of completing their reconnaissance, and an outside chance of reaching Haramosh I.

6

THE CLIMB TO CAMP IV

Next morning at Camp III, a warm yellow light permeated the canvas of the Meade tent, giving Jillott and Culbert the impression of a bright sunny dawn. But when they emerged from the tent they saw that the weather was dull and threatening and that snow had fallen in the night. The illusion of a sunny morning had come from the yellow canvas of the tent itself.

The idea of these colourful tents was to make them stand out well against the snow from a distance. A dull canvas would be easily absorbed into the panorama of snow. It was the same with their high-altitude clothing. Fully dressed in their windproof suits, canvas overboots, hoods and goggles, their individualism disappeared. But the brightly coloured windproof suits served a dual purpose – that of distinguishing one man from another and of showing up well against the snow.

In their sleeping bags, or fully dressed and on the move, they were rarely cold, in spite of the extremely low temperatures of as much as thirty degrees below zero and the piercing wind. It was at the end of a day's climbing, when icy crampons, frozen to the boots, had to be untied with unfeeling fingers, and when the boots themselves, stiff as boards with frost, had to be dragged off, that the cold attacked them; or first thing in the morning, when the warm sleeping bag had to be abandoned and frozen boots pulled on again, for the first plunge into the icy air-bath outside. A man might lie in his sleeping bag for two or three hours in real pain, wondering how long he could hold on to yesterday's food and drink.

It was remarkable how completely snug they were inside their sleeping bags, sheltered from the wind by the flimsy tent wall. There wasn't even any draught. Several feet of snow might build up outside and almost smother the tent, and they would be unaware of it till morning. Even then, their only clue might be a strange oppressive silence, when even the sound of the wind on the canvas was deadened.

Jillott and Culbert were soon back inside the tent with the Primus roaring. Both, however, had slept badly and were feeling the effects of the altitude. They had the usual breakfast of porridge, Ryvita and marmalade, washed down with plenty of tea, and they then started off down to the loads left by the Hunzas yesterday. The track, which the previous day had looked like a conduit cut for a pipeline, was now only just visible, being almost completely filled with fresh snow.

The trip down took only half an hour, but the long plod uphill on the way back took double that time. They lingered in camp for a further hour, making fresh tea, and then descended to the dump for a second time. About halfway down they saw four figures appearing over the lip of the upper snow basin, just emerging from the icefall. Soon they recognised Hamilton and three of the Hunzas, on the way up with loads from Camp II.

They got all the loads, the previous day's and that day's, through to Camp III, and then Streather and Emery appeared, having made a late start after eating a huge lunch at Camp II. Both were completely recovered and were to remain at Camp III. Hamilton took the porters on down, planning to return the following day with fresh loads. Hamilton would then stay at Camp III with one porter, sending the other porters back to Camp II. Thus the remaining climbers would be free to establish at least one higher camp and make an all-out attempt on Haramosh II.

Next day, however, the weather was so bad that little movement was possible. The track was still faintly visible, but fresh snow had buried all the stores recently brought up. Streather and Emery spent the day clearing the camp while Jillott and Culbert dug again for the lost food dump. Unless they could find these stores, they wouldn't be able to establish more than one higher camp without leaving this one dangerously short.

5 September brought a fine day at last, and all four climbers moved off together for a reconnaissance of the snow slope leading up to the right towards Haramosh II. First they had to climb the gentle gradient of the Haramosh glacier to a col which marked the glacier head, directly below the steep snow slope. They were making the track through lightly lying snow about two feet deep which made the going fairly hard, but they reached the col in forty-five minutes. They were now about 400 feet above Camp III, and the mountain panorama was magnificent. Malubiting and Rakaposhi stood out clearly, and down the Haramosh glacier they looked back at the graceful peaks beyond the Chogo Lungma. Haramosh itself was still hidden, but as they reached the col the cloud ahead of them cleared and away to their left they had their first peep into the Stak Valley 6,000 feet below, falling away sheer from the head of the Haramosh glacier. This valley was a bewildering palette of black rock, steel-blue ice and snow, and green trees. The glacier itself was dirty and moraine-covered, with a shrunken, hollow bed and high lateral terraces thick with pine trees, but the valley as a whole and the peaks beyond offered a fine prospect.

They turned towards the snow slope leading up to the high ground that lay between them and the north-east ridge, and began the ascent, taking turns to lead. Again there was a two-foot layer of soft fresh snow to plug through. The slope was fairly gradual at first, but steepened as they climbed, reaching fifty-five degrees towards the top. Above them the way seemed to be barred by two ice cliffs, one slightly lower and to the left of the other. Both these ice cliffs faced slightly away from the slope and therefore did not threaten it. When they reached the top of the slope they found themselves on the edge of a large crevasse which ran between the two ice cliffs, cutting them off from the upper ice cliff altogether. The top of the ice cliff on their left formed part of the lower, downside wall of this crevasse.

Having reached the lip of the crevasse and satisfied themselves that there was no way in which they could gain the top of the upper ice cliff, they turned to the left and traversed along the lower lip of the crevasse. This lower lip quickly developed into a small ridge which led up to the top of the lower ice cliff. On their left the ground now fell away vertically some hundred feet or so down the face of the ice cliff and then very steeply for a further 6,000 feet down the mountain flank to the Stak Valley, which itself fell right away to the Indus. And immediately on their right was a frothy snow cornice which curled over the lower lip of the crevasse. The route ahead was nothing more than a narrow neck of snow, on one side of which was the sheer drop down the mountainside and on the other the overhang of snow cornice underneath which was the crevasse.

Crossing this narrow neck of snow would always have its hazards, but it would be safe enough provided they took proper care. And at the far end of the neck of snow, not more than 150 feet distant, they could see that the crevasse curved away to the right, allowing the snow surface to broaden out into a shelf on the flank of the mountain which would make an ideal site for Camp IV.

Already, on the snow slope, occasional small crevasses had forced them to rope up, and they had had to abandon their plan to change the lead every few minutes. Emery had led up the last part of the slope to the ice cliffs, but now Streather took over. The snow here was still soft enough to take a kicked step, and he began to stamp his way across the narrow neck of snow, belayed by Culbert, keeping as far to the downside of the neck as possible to avoid the overhanging cornice. Every few steps he jabbed at the cornice with his ice axe, sending it falling away like rotten plaster deep into the crevasse. Moving carefully, belaying each other in turn, they all reached the plateau at the far end.

The climb from Camp III had taken them four hours. They dropped their packs on the snow plateau and for the first time took in the magnificent scenery. From the top of the snow slope they had been able to look down a thousand feet to the Haramosh glacier and trace their tracks all the way back to Camp III. Now they moved on from the snow plateau for a few minutes to gain the foot of a small spur which led on to the ridge above their new camp site. From here they had a clear view of the nearest of the three peaks that formed the complex of Haramosh II, and beyond it, to the right, they could see into the head of the Kutwal Valley. They had come right round behind the north-east ridge leading up to Haramosh II from the La, and were now approaching Haramosh II from the east.

They had reached a height at which, in every direction except where Haramosh barred the way, they were above the surrounding ridges, so that they could stare out at the boundless Himalaya, hundreds and hundreds of peaks at eye level stretching away into the blue distance, giving them a sudden sensation of having climbed to a great height, making the soles of their feet tingle with a pleasurable vertigo. They had to look down and stamp on the firm snow to counteract the feeling of insecurity.

This was the view that they had come to see, the panorama that only the mountaineer saw. It was as though they had gone to the top of a high building and looked out across the limitless and haphazard but strangely uniform roofs of a vast city, with here and there some great landmark on which to rest the eye – the dome of a museum, the pinnacle of a monument, the campanile of a cathedral. They could see in some directions for eighty to a hundred miles, but even so there was much that was still hidden from them. This was but a small corner of the grandeur and magnificence they would see from the summit.

The route ahead towards Haramosh II looked quite favourable. They would have to zigzag back and forth to avoid a number of apparent obstacles, but there was nothing in view that couldn't be negotiated.

They returned in high spirits to Camp III, immensely encouraged by the progress made and the glimpse of grandeur to come. It had been their most successful day's climbing for two and a half weeks, since the time when they had dumped the stores above the icefall ready to site Camp III. Streather was only too conscious how much they had all needed a little success. Frustrations such as they had endured were enough to damp anyone's enthusiasm. Even for him the last week or so had been little more than a duty, the duty of seeing the expedition through. Yet somehow their basic regard for one another had survived the strain of discomfort, altitude, proximity, inactivity and frustration. It had been a good idea for the whole high-altitude party to climb together. The experience had finally cemented them into a team.

Soon after they got back to Camp III, which took them only an hour, Hamilton arrived from Camp II with Nadir and Rustam. Dhilap Shah and Johar were ill. Johar had started out with them, but had been forced to turn back.

This was a particularly severe blow as he had been carrying food, of which there was a shortage at Camp III as the food dump had still not been found. The plan had been for Nadir to stay up at Camp III with Hamilton, and he had therefore been carrying his personal kit. But they couldn't send Rustam back through the icefall alone, so Nadir had to go with him, lugging his personal kit all the way back to Camp II. It was a complete waste of a carry; unfortunately no one had thought of exchanging Nadir's load for Johar's when Johar had had to turn back.

The weather deteriorated that evening, the snow starting even before they had finished their light-hearted descent from Camp IV. The plan was for all five climbers to make a carry up the steep snow slope next day and establish Culbert and Emery at Camp IV, but the weather in the morning was bad again – snow and wind and cloud combining to make a thoroughly grim day.

Jillott was about early in readiness to get away, and Streather, too, was determined to get through to Camp IV that day if it was at all possible.

The previous day's success would soon turn sour on them if they were unable to follow it up. The pendulum would swing even harder the other way.

Streather was convinced that, now they were almost through the first week in September, the weather must soon become more stable. They had only seven or eight days' climbing left. Plugging their way through the fresh snow up to Camp IV would be pretty exhausting, and would be more than perhaps he would normally feel like attempting, but it didn't really matter if they wore themselves out in the next few days. There was nothing to save themselves for now. And what weighed with him perhaps more than anything was the morale factor. He had to give his party action; he had to foster in them some hope of achievement in the next few days.

The chances of reaching Haramosh I were now virtually non-existent, and it was doubtful even if they could reach Haramosh II. But he was determined to give his party every chance of reaching a point from which they could view the trough dividing the two summits, to decide whether it was practicable as a route. It was the sort of lowering of sights which he had always known might be forced on them, but it would at least give them the satisfaction of having completed a worthwhile reconnaissance.

They started up towards the col at the head of the Haramosh glacier with heavy loads, and it was hard and unpleasant work, with a strong wind driving snow into their faces and with the previous day's tracks covered by fresh snow. Culbert led all the way to the col at the head of the glacier, his ice axe stretched out before him like a mine detector, prodding ahead to find the firm snow of the old track. He excelled at this hard, rhythmic plugging through deep snow. Streather took over at the col, and they took turns up the snow slope, roping up when they reached the big crevasse. It took them over four hours to reach the snow plateau. They levelled a site for the yellow Meade tent, and then, since it was getting late, Streather led off across the narrow neck of snow back to Camp III, followed by Jillott and Hamilton, leaving Culbert and Emery to pitch their frozen tent alone.

Visibility was bad and the blanket of mist and cloud seemed to isolate Culbert and Emery still further at Camp IV. They inflated their lilos, sat in the tent and cooked and ate their supper, and got into their sleeping bags soon after dark. The snow was falling heavily on the yellow canvas above them.

7

THE SNOW CAVE

When Culbert and Emery awoke next morning at Camp IV the plateau was wrapped in thick cloud and the tent was half-covered in snow. Their horizon was limited to the start of the narrow neck of snow leading down to the ice cliffs below them, and a vague outline of the slope up towards Haramosh II above. There was no chance of progress that day.

Culbert cooked breakfast while Emery got to work clearing the snow away from the tent. The weather showed no improvement at midday and the two men spent a lazy, friendly day, chatting and reading, secure in the comfort of their sleeping bags. It was impossible to move far either up or down, and there was no chance of anyone getting through from Camp III.

About five o'clock that afternoon, Emery thought he heard a shout from outside the tent. Both men got up, pulled on their boots, and hurried outside. There was no sign of anyone, and the weather was just as thick, but again they heard a shout. The sound seemed to come from the direction of the ice cliffs. It looked as though the others had somehow managed to force their way up.

The two men crossed the narrow neck of snow and stood at the top of the ice cliffs, peering down the slope. Below them stood a very aggrieved party: Streather, Jillott and Hamilton.

'Why didn't you make the track down to us?' called Jillott. 'We've been five and a half hours getting through. It would have been easier for you, coming down.'

'Didn't you hear our shouts?' asked Streather. 'We've been shouting and blowing whistles for the last half hour.'

'We never thought you'd attempt it,' said Emery.

He realised that they had reckoned without Jillott's determination to press on, and Streather's reluctance to overrule him. In spite of themselves they both felt a bit sheepish. Privately, they felt that the others must have been mad to make the trip under these conditions, but they'd got through and so were really above criticism. They began to examine their own position. Were they blameless? Had it really been too bad; shouldn't they perhaps have made the route down to the ice cliffs at least? On the whole they felt like standing their ground – it had been an appalling day, with visibility almost nil, a great deal of new snow, and still more snow falling all the time. But they understood how the others must feel, fighting their way through to a pair of climbers who were sitting it out in the sack.

Streather's party all had heavy loads, mostly food, and Culbert and Emery took these on to Camp IV while the others went down. Very little more was said on either side. Streather promptly forgot the incident, but it worried Culbert and Emery, and it lingered in their minds.

The return trip to Camp III took only forty minutes. Camp IV was now well stocked, with sufficient food to support the whole party for at least a week. If Streather was worried about anything it was Camp III. The porters had been unable to get through from Camp II, they still hadn't found the lost food dump, and they had rather denuded Camp III in order to establish Camp IV. They badly needed another strong carry through from Camp II.

It snowed heavily all that night and all next morning, and movement was out of the question. The three climbers at Camp III had spread themselves out now, each having a tent to himself. Jillott, who had been suffering from a sore throat the previous day, had taken two sleeping tablets overnight, but he still had a disturbed night and his throat seemed to be worse. He finally awoke just as it was getting light, and was aware at once that heavy snow must have fallen in the night. The roof of his tent was caved in on both sides with the weight of it.

He unfastened the back door of the tent, just behind his head, and opened the funnel inwards. The snow outside had packed in hard against the tent wall, and as he pulled the canvas towards him a few grains of snow fell into the tent. He struggled upwards out of his sleeping bag. There was hardly room to kneel on the air bed, so low was the roof under the weight of snow. He reached up and banged his hand upwards and outwards against the sloping roof with the object of dislodging the snow, but the level of snow outside was evidently too high for it to slide off. His banging had no effect but to shower drops of condensed moisture down on to his sleeping bag.

He closed the back door of the tent and started to settle down into his sleeping bag again. His throat was extremely sore and he decided not to make a move just yet. He might as well wait for the others. Then, glancing down at the front entrance facing him, he saw to his dismay that snow had poured in through a small tear in the tent door. A drift several inches deep had formed inside the tent and over his feet.

He would have to do something about this straight away. Fortunately he had put his anorak jacket over the foot of his sleeping bag, and this had taken nearly all the snow. It was thoroughly soaked, but the sleeping bag itself was dry. He arranged the tent cloth around the tear so as to stop any more snow coming in. Now he had to get rid of the snow that had already come in. To do this he would have to open the tent funnel, but the level of the snow outside was well above this. He untied the funnel carefully, but as he opened it a shower of loose powder snow poured into the tent like a shovelful of salt.

'Damn!' He scooped the snow up in his hands and tried to push it out through the funnel, but it slid straight back into the tent. Contact with the snow had chilled his hands painfully and made them sting fiercely. He looked around for some sort of scoop.

There was a dish in the corner of the tent that he had had his soup in last night. He grabbed it and began scooping up the snow and pouring it into the funnel, but the snow still slid back and froze his hands. God! He put on a glove, but it was icily wet.

Then he had an idea. With his gloved hand he began to make the snow inside the tent into snowballs. Then he reached through the funnel and pressed the snow outside until he had made a hollow. Now he stuffed the snowballs through the funnel into the hollow. Soon he had cleared the tent completely.

He heaved himself back into his sleeping bag and lay there exhausted, watching the condensation drip from the roof on to his sleeping bag, too exhausted by his efforts to care. Presently he heard his name called from outside. It was Streather.

'Are you all right, Bernard?'

'Hallo, Tony. Yes, I'm all right.'

'Thank goodness for that. Your tent's completely buried. I've just crawled out of mine.'

'I had quite a drift inside the tent,' said Jillott. 'I've been clearing it out.'

'How's your throat?'

'Still a bit sore.'

He could hear the dull crunch of Tony's boots outside. He must be digging out his tent. Then the crunch seemed to come nearer. Soon he saw the front of his tent move slightly. Tony was clearing the snow from the doorway. Perhaps he ought to get out and help. His sore throat gave him an excuse.

It was still snowing. He lay where he was, with a bad conscience, writing up his diary. The condensation went on dripping from the tent roof.

He heard Streather calling to Hamilton. 'Where did you put the snow shovel when you came in yesterday, Scott?' Hamilton, evidently out of earshot, made no reply. 'It's by his tent – just this side,' called Jillott.

So Streather must have been digging all this time with his plate. In spite of their differences, he could feel nothing but admiration for the man.

He caught a glimpse of Streather's red anorak through the tear in the tent. The snow was still streaking down. His hands were very cold. He put his diary away and thrust his hands back into the warmth of his sleeping bag.

He began to feel hungry. Some time later Hamilton pushed a flask of tea through the tear in the tent. He drank two cups and ate some dry Ryvita biscuits and the only glucose tablet he had left. Then he smoked a cigarette. It was damp and it took three matches to get it alight. He enjoyed it, so his throat must be getting better. As he exhaled the smoke, it filled the tent with haze, mixing with the water vapour in the roof and creeping in small smoke-avalanches down the sodden walls. It was still snowing heavily outside.

He began to regret the previous day's carry to Camp IV. It had left them short of food here, and while they were struggling up to Camp IV they could have gone down to Camp II to get some decent food. He was determined to go down to Camp II for food as soon as the snow stopped.

Later Hamilton brought him some Ovaltine tablets, and at midday Streather brought more tea and a fresh packet of Ryvita. 'You and Scott divide it in two,' he said.

'How about you?'

'I've still got about six left from yesterday.'

'But surely I'd better divide this into three?'

'No, it's all right. What I've got left over will do me. I'm fine.'

Jillott supposed that there must be some porridge about somewhere, and he wished Streather would make some. But he couldn't very well ask, not having done anything to help. Probably Streather was saving it for the evening. He was the perfect ascetic.

By mid-afternoon, Jillott felt he could no longer bear the snow pressing down the roof of the tent to within a few inches of his nose. It was impossible to raise his head properly to read or write. He zipped his sleeping bag down and crawled to the other end of the tent. It was like squirming down a pothole tunnel. He pulled his anorak jacket and trousers over his eiderdown clothing and struggled into his boots. When he emerged from the tent, the white world outside struck his eyes painfully and he put on his snow goggles. The other two had finished digging out their tents and were some distance away digging for the missing dump of stores. It didn't look as if they'd found anything.

He dug the snow away from his tent and then joined the others. The three men spent the rest of the day digging for the lost dump. They dug a series of trenches four to five feet deep and then probed about with their ice axes, but they could tell that they were still not down to the original level. Then they dug an enormous cave. Still they hit nothing.

Next day the weather was just the same. There was no chance of anyone getting through from Camp II with the kitbag of food that had been left behind last time. Soon they would be forced to go down. Streather decided that they must try to get through to Camp II at the first sign of a break in the weather. He disliked leaving this camp empty with two climbers at Camp IV, but they had more than enough food up there, and since they must certainly be confined to their tent they couldn't come to much harm. He, Jillott and Hamilton would be able to find their way through the icefall to Camp II, and they would come straight back with loads as soon as possible.

While they were waiting for some small improvement in the weather, they continued digging for the dump of stores. By the end of their second day of confinement at Camp III, the whole area looked like the site of Roman excavations.

Next day, 10 September, the weather was still dull and threatening and the cloud was low, but it wasn't actually snowing, and this at least was an improvement. All three climbers had trudged between Camps II and III many times and they were confident of finding their way. They tidied up the camp and set out for Camp II at eleven o'clock.

Soon they found themselves up to their hips in snow, virtually cutting a trench down the glacier slope. They moved extremely slowly, taking it in turns to lead. Low cloud and mist obscured the mountain ridges on either side of the glacier and reduced visibility in places to less than fifty yards. Their tracks quickly disappeared in the mist behind them, making it more and more difficult for them to be sure that they were going forward in a straight line.

They went on ploughing through the soft snow, more than waist-deep now, peering through the mist to try to catch a glimpse of some remembered rock formation to the left or right. They changed the leadership frequently, each leader being forced to drop his rucksack, make the track for a few minutes, and then go back for his rucksack, joining on to the tail end of the column to let the next man take over. Their rate of progress was often no more than a hundred yards an hour.

Sometimes they thought they recognised the fluting of a ridge or the outline of a rock pinnacle, and they would be convinced that they were moving in the right direction. But the test would come when they reached the icefall. They had to find the ladder across the deep crevasse, and it might be covered in snow; unless they were well on track they might miss it altogether.

The light was deceptive, leaden and flat, almost eerie, throwing no shadows, making the whole area seem strangely unfamiliar. By mid-afternoon there was still no sign of the icefall. A strong wind was blowing the loose surface snow about, making visibility even worse, and they began to realise that they were so unsure of their position as to be virtually lost.

It was six o'clock when they reached the top of the icefall. They were still getting occasional glimpses of the north-east ridge to their left and of the rock ridge to their right, but these glimpses were no help in judging distance. There was no sign of the ladder. They stood about uncertainly above the icefall, trying to recognise some feature that would tell them whether the ladder lay up the lateral slope of the glacier to their left or down to their right. But even if they found the ladder, they would still be faced with the prospect of crossing the icefall as darkness fell.

It seemed that they had several choices: they could return quite safely to Camp III and try again the next day; they could keep on trying to get through to Camp II, but be prepared to bivouac for the night on the way if necessary, probably in the icefall; or they could bivouac where they were and look for the ladder in the morning, when it ought to be easy to find. Streather didn't fancy a bivouac in the icefall, but he was equally reluctant to negative much of their hard slogging by returning to Camp III. He decided that they should bivouac where they were.

'We'll dig a snow cave,' he told them. 'The Norwegians go in for them in a big way.' Jillott and Hamilton looked doubtful. 'The last three high camps on Tirich Mir were snow caves,' he added.

The other two looked more enthusiastic. 'We've had enough practice at digging, anyway,' said Jillott. 'Let's get cracking.'

Streather took the snow shovel and began digging at an angle into the snow. Jillott and Hamilton grabbed plates and cleared the snow away as Streather threw it out. In order to make the tunnelling easier, Streather chose a piece of slightly rising ground. All he had to do was to dig into the slight rise and he was soon several feet below the surface. When the rising ground was about six feet above his tunnel, he began to dig first to the left and then to the right until he had opened out a T-shaped shelter, the long upward stroke of the T forming the entrance, and the horizontal stroke, some six feet below the surface, forming a cave. Then they dragged their packs down the tunnel, spread out their air mattresses and sleeping bags, and lit a Primus. The roof of the cave was curved in an arc, like a tube tunnel, so that as the snow melted with the warmth of the Primus and of their bodies, it followed the arc of the roof and did not drip down on to them. Streather stuck a plate into the cave wall to act as a shelf, and fixed a candle on it. Soon the candle was making a tiny chimney for itself in the cave roof.

They scraped chunks of snow off the walls and melted it down for water, and then ate a meal of dates and sweets. The cave was warmer in some ways than a tent. They stuffed their rucksacks into the foot of the tunnel where the cave opened out, and they were completely protected from the wind. However cold it got outside, it would never be much below freezing inside the cave. There was sufficient headroom for them to be able to sit up and eat their supper, and there was no danger of the snow caving in. Even if it did, it wouldn't be very deep and they would be able to struggle to the surface.

They all slept well at what they facetiously called 'Camp two and a half', and next morning they emerged from the cave into bright sunshine and a beautiful day. But the shifting breakers of the icefall had so changed its aspect that they were still not sure where they were. The most likely thing seemed to be that they had strayed to the right the previous day because of the left-to-right slope of the glacier, and that the ladder was higher up towards the north-east ridge. They packed their sleeping bags and gear and began to traverse to their left. At first they were confident that they would find the ladder within a few minutes, but soon they were wandering about almost aimlessly, with no clear idea where they were. The snow was still waist-deep and their progress was slow.

By midday they had still not found the ladder, and they began to feel hungry and dispirited. Streather had withheld some of the food in case of a further delay on the route, and he produced this now. He was not unduly concerned about their own position, but he was anxious not to leave Camp IV unsupported for long. Somehow they must get through to Camp II today, so as to be back in Camp III within another day or so. After a discussion with Jillott he decided that the ladder must be completely buried under the fresh snow and that it was a waste of time going on prodding about in the hope of finding it. They must find some other way to bridge the big crevasse, and then try to find the route through the icefall.

They found an insecure-looking ice bridge across the big crevasse, and Streather led the way across, belayed from above by both Jillott and Hamilton. The ice bridge was about five feet thick and was covered by a layer of snow, into which Streather sank deeply several times. Chunks of ice fell away from the underside of the bridge, but it held. Jillott took over the lead in the icefall. Longer in the leg than Streather, he was more effective in the deep snow. He had to find an entirely new route, twisting and turning round the maze of crevasses, making detours to avoid overhanging ice pinnacles, expecting all the time to fall into a hidden crevasse. The route was extremely broken and the whole structure of the icefall seemed to have changed. It was as though some giant hand had shaken it all up together, like a lumpy feather bed, leaving it even more angular and contorted than before.

They crossed a very narrow snow crest and then found themselves dropping down a steep snow slope. Now at last they knew where they were. This was the steep snow slope that led down into the basin just above Camp II. Even this seemed to have changed. At the bottom of the slope to the right was a huge crevasse, and to their left was a great hole in an ice projection. They steered a middle course carefully so that if they happened to fall they would slide between these hazards and finish up safely in the snow basin. Hamilton led the way, while Streather paid the rope out carefully, keeping it almost taut. Then Jillott followed Hamilton down, and lastly came Streather, belayed from below, so that if he slipped he would fall the full length of the rope beyond them before the rope pulled taut; this was the sort of belay that seldom held. Hamilton slipped twice, but each time was held from above.

In the bottom of the snow basin was a great deal of new snow debris, but this avalanched snow was crisp and hard and they crossed it easily.

The sun was bright again now, and their spirits were high. When they got to Camp II, only the two top corners of the green tent were showing – a pair of ears protruding from the snow. With the recent bad weather the Hunzas had gone down, but they had left a pan of dehydrated vegetables already prepared, and Jillott and Hamilton began cooking while Streather dug out the tent. The stores, too, were buried, and the tarpaulin cover had been torn by the weight of snow. By the time Streather had finished, the sky had turned to purple and the stars had appeared. It was a cold night, but they climbed into their sleeping bags happily. The next day they would thoroughly remake the route through the icefall, and they would be back at Camp III by the following day at the latest.

If this weather lasted, Culbert and Emery would be making progress above Camp IV, so that, in the three or four days' climbing remaining to them, they might still be able to reach some vantage point on Haramosh II. Everything depended on what groundwork could be laid by Culbert and Emery in the next day or so.

Streather and Jillott spent the whole of the next day clearing the snow around Camp II and remaking the track through the icefall, while Hamilton did the domestic chores in camp. They found the old route, now under four or five feet of snow, and eventually located the ladder. The crevasse had widened considerably and the end of the ladder was only just lodged on the upper lip. They secured it again carefully and then marked its position, tying two flagpoles together this time to give more height, and flying from the top a piece of the torn tarpaulin, bright orange in colour, that they had brought specially with them from Camp II. Now the position would still be easy to find even under another six feet of snow.

They were able to see clearly where they had gone wrong the previous day. They had evidently hit the top of the icefall too far to the left, probably through over-correcting against the lateral slope of the glacier; and they had then turned the wrong way. They found the spot where they had hit the icefall ; it was only fifty yards from the ladder. Had they turned right they would have found it at once.

Next day, 13 September, they returned to Camp III. This would be their last time through the icefall in this direction. The first Jeep was coming to pick them up in Sussi in six days' time. It would take them at least a day to get from base camp to Sussi, and another two days to get off the mountain, possibly three. After today, the most they could possibly look forward to was another two days' climbing. And of these two days, the first would be spent on the route between Camp III and Camp IV, where the snow would certainly be waist-deep again. That meant that when they finally reached Camp IV there would be only one day's climbing left.

How far had Culbert and Emery managed to make the route above Camp IV? Throughout the day, plodding steadily up to Camp III, they kept their eyes fixed on the smooth snow slopes leading up to Haramosh II. And in the afternoon they were rewarded by the sight of two minute figures high on a ridge above Camp IV.

'Look! Rae and John!' They pointed wildly and shouted excitedly. 'And they're still going up!' It was true. The line of their tracks was clear behind them, but ahead of them the snow was unmarked. Slowly they were ploughing their way upwards.

For three men who had spent the last six days hindered and frustrated between Camps II and III, after weeks of similar frustrations, it was the most encouraging, heart-warming sight they could possibly see. It was an animated little party which moved into Camp III that night. The reconnaissance would be completed yet.

8

EMERY AND THE CREVASSE

Streather, Jillott and Hamilton had made their last carry from Camp III up to Camp IV on 7 September. For the next seven days, Culbert and Emery were isolated at Camp IV. At first the weather was so bad that they were unable to move more than a few yards from the tent, and then only for the purpose of digging away the fresh snow. Sometimes this operation alone took them several hours. Soon their daily digging left them sheltered in a hollow, with high banks of snow all round the tent, which was completely hidden from view at five yards distance. Visibility was no more than ten yards or so for days on end, and they didn't even have to consider the possibility of the others trying to get through from Camp III.

These two men, thrown into protracted and comfortless proximity, with nothing to divert their minds except talking and reading, found a great companionship and thoroughly enjoyed their enforced isolation. Culbert always found it easy to relax. Emery, during the past few weeks, had come to acquire something of Culbert's and Streather's view of mountains, and his temperament had never been altogether unsuited to enforced idleness.

Culbert, outwardly shy and reserved, found that he could talk without embarrassment to Emery about Greta, of his memories of the past and hopes for the future. Emery recognised the sensitivity and warmth that lay beneath Culbert's tough exterior, and he in turn found himself able to talk easily about his own emotional attachments. But for the most part their talk was of superficial things, of matters concerned with their own personal comfort and survival at high altitude in bad weather. They were too near the eternal things to talk much about them, and such things as philosophies and attitudes to life were taken on trust.

On 11 September, four days after Streather, Jillott and Hamilton had made their carry, the mist and cloud that had enveloped Camp IV ever since then began to clear a little towards afternoon. Remembering the lesson they had learnt last time, Culbert and Emery decided that they had better make the track down to the ice cliffs. Having done that, they would be able to look down the slope to Camp III to see if there were any signs of movement. It was extremely unlikely that anyone would get up to them, but after the last occasion they felt that they could hardly be certain. In any case, although conditions were bad, they were only too glad of an opportunity to regain the initiative and do something constructive.

They quickly covered the short distance across the snow plateau between the camp and the blade of snow that led past the crevasse. From the plateau they looked down into the crevasse, noting its cavernous depths, fascinated by a sharp ice pinnacle that seemed to grow out of the depths and force its way up into the jaws of the crevasse in the form of a shark's tooth, a single, impressive tusk in the mouth of a monster. The whole area round the crevasse was swollen with a surfeit of new snow.

Culbert took a belay with his ice axe into good firm snow at the edge of the snow plateau, and Emery prepared to lead off across the narrow neck of snow. He studied the relative dangers of the cornice on his left, which had built up during the recent falls of snow to a dangerous height, and the steep slope of the mountain, falling away almost sheer to his right. The light was improving, and he could see a faint shadow in the snow which was all that remained of the old track. From the plateau it seemed to him that the cornice presented the greater danger, and he took a line slightly lower than the old track to make doubly sure.

The slope of the mountain was extremely steep on the low line he had taken, perhaps as much as sixty degrees, and he felt his way cautiously forward. Now he was on the slope he could no longer see into the crevasse, which was completely hidden by the towering cornice that rose high above him on his left. Sometimes, where the mountain slope steepened, he was forced to flirt with the danger of the cornice, but he still kept below the old track.

He was about eight feet below the cornice, but he wished he had some means of judging the overhang. Every step he took he jabbed first with his ice axe, both in front of him and at the cornice.

He had travelled about two-thirds of the distance across the blade of snow, and he had reached a point where the mountain slope fell away sharply and the cornice rose to a height of ten or twelve feet above him. He stopped in his tracks, jabbing the cornice with his ice axe to try to establish where the feathery, unstable part began. He remembered the picture that he had impressed on his mind when planning his track, an imaginary dotted line for his mind to follow, and he was sure he was on the right line. Then suddenly, as he jabbed again with his ice axe, the treacherous cornice fell away and the snow on which he was standing opened like a trap-door and he felt himself falling, falling feet first in a flurry of snow, down into the bottomless chasm of the crevasse.

He had no thought at first other than of surprise and annoyance. Then he remembered the belay. That was his only hope now, and the question thundered into his mind. Would the belay hold?

He must have been about seventy feet from Rae Culbert when he fell. Seventy feet of rope. Culbert would have the rope fairly taut, and he wondered why there was no jerk, why he still seemed to be falling. Then he realised that he was swinging back towards Culbert, swinging deeper and deeper into the crevasse. As he swung, the rope was cutting through the cornice like string through cheese, showering him with snow. He had swung back almost to the point of the belay. In a moment his weight would pull the rope taut and he would know whether the belay was going to hold.

The fact that he had been waiting anxiously for the jerk made it all the more shocking when it came. It was instant arrest, shattering in its severity; from full speed to full stop. Half of him seemed to be still careering along the chasm. It was a moment before he could be sure what had happened. The belay must have held.

The pressure of the rope on his chest was suffocating and he kicked out until he gained a foothold on a narrow snow ledge. Now he loosened the rope a little from under his rasped armpits and breathed deeply.

So far his attention had been fixed on the near wall of the crevasse as he fought for a foothold. Now he took stock of his position. He still had his ice axe: somehow he had held on to it during the fall. Below him the crevasse continued downwards in a dark crack that had no visible ending. Looking up, he could see the rope snaking up against the wall of the crevasse, fifty or sixty feet above him, disappearing beyond an overhang near the top. There was plenty of light in the crevasse, and straight above him he could see a thin strip of sky, unattainable but somehow incredibly close. It was like looking up through a crack in a barn roof.

He began to shout for Culbert. 'Rae! I'm here! I'm OK! Are you all right? Rae!' His voice reverberated around him and rumbled in the chasm beneath his feet. He shouted again, but there was still no answer. His ears fought to catch the merest decibel of sound. But there was nothing.

He began to wonder what had happened to Culbert. If he was on the other end of the rope he couldn't be more than a hundred feet away. Surely he would have given an answering shout and perhaps given a tug at the rope? Where else could he be? Perhaps after all the belay hadn't held, and Cuthbert had thrown himself down the mountain slope to hold the fall, so that the rope now lay over the fulcrum of the crevasse lip, with the two of them suspended on either side like the weights of a clock. It was possible that Culbert had done this anyway, just in case, and that he was now working his way back to the belay point.

How was he going to get out? The first possibility that occurred to him was to climb straight up the rope. He had one prusik loop with him, and Culbert had another and could lower it down the rope. He could use these loops as steps, advancing first in one and then the other, bringing the lower one forward each time, gaining height up the rope. The loops were so constructed that when you put your weight on them they gripped the climbing rope tightly, but otherwise slipped up or down the rope easily.

But he would be climbing straight up the ice wall, which would be very tiring and would take a long time. At the top, too, there was the overhang to be surmounted. It looked extremely difficult and it would be a terrific strain on Culbert as well as on himself.

The second possibility, less direct but perhaps less difficult, was to continue in the direction in which he had originally set out, travelling inside the crevasse instead of along the lip. The ground fell away slightly down towards the ice cliffs, so that by keeping his present level within the crevasse and working his way along the wall, he wouldn't have very far to climb out at the far end. It might take a long time, but there must be about two and a half hours' daylight left and it ought to be enough.

He shouted again to Culbert, and this time heard his answering call. Emery had completely recovered his breath now and he realised that his voice was much stronger than before.

'I'm going to try to work my way along the crevasse and climb out at the ice cliffs,' he shouted. 'I shall need some more rope.'

'Right.' Emery's weight on the rope had dug the embedded ice axe in even more firmly, and after testing it again Culbert untied himself, secured the rope to the ice axe, and went back to Camp IV. There were three lengths of hemp rope, but they were all frozen stiff. He uncoiled one of them, brought it back to the belay point, and attached it to the nylon rope with which they had been climbing. Emery, alone in the crevasse, seemed to wait a long time.

'OK, John, she's right.'

Emery realised that the snow he was standing on was not debris but an island in the crevasse. The crevasse seemed to be narrower here than he remembered, and then he realised that the wall of ice on his left was not the upper wall of the crevasse but the ice pinnacle which rose in the centre of the crevasse to form a shark's tooth at the top. He was actually on a sort of island supported by the lower wall and the ice pinnacle. Looking along the crevasse in the direction he wanted to go, he saw that directly in front of him was an arch of snow, and that there was ample room for him to climb through.

Beyond the arch he found that the crevasse wall and the ice pinnacle were too far apart for him to jam his body between them so as to proceed safely, and he took a line close to the ice pinnacle, climbing on snow debris. It seemed soft and fairly deep, and it held him for the most part, but in places it was obviously not very firm. He used his ice axe as a probe, and when the surface ahead seemed unsafe he jammed himself as best he could, using the ice pinnacle on his left and firm snow debris on his right. In this way he progressed slowly but in a straight line.

The right-hand wall of the crevasse was now beginning to slope down towards him, and he realised that he had come past the ice cliffs and that above him now was the ridge running down to the top of the slope leading to Camp III. But the crevasse wall was still about thirty feet above him, and it was unlikely that he could climb out here as the wall at this point seemed very unstable. To his left, the ice pinnacle was gradually getting smaller and smaller until just ahead it fell away to nothing; the snow debris gave out and the crevasse opened up and fell away directly in front of him. He had gone as far as he possibly could in a straight line.

The only way out seemed to lie in a wide detour to the left. This would carry him up sloping snow debris towards the left-hand, upper crevasse wall. He could then sweep round in a half-circle which would eventually bring him out at the end of the crevasse.

He had hardly begun this detour when he realised that the rope was pulling taut. He must be 200 feet from the belay point. They would need another length of rope. He shouted back to Culbert, and again Culbert went back to Camp IV for more rope. Then he continued on the detour. He was now on 300 feet of rope, and if he slipped there was no telling where he might end.

He was climbing on snow which seemed stable enough in places but which he could never be sure of, and at one point he reached a definite extension of the crevasse, a sort of crevasse within a crevasse, which baffled him completely.

There was no way round it and there seemed to be no way of climbing across. At length, stabbing his ice axe in the snow as far ahead as possible to give him a leverage, and using a technique of even distribution of the body over the whole crevassed surface, he swam across at the narrowest point, his stomach and chest pressed flat into the snow, his eyes forced to look down beneath him where the crevasse fell away into the depths. But he got across safely, and it proved to be the only point of real difficulty on the detour. He continued round in a half-circle which eventually brought him to the lower end of the crevasse. By climbing up a short, easy wall, he was out.

Now he had to climb up the ridge to the top of the ice cliff and make his way back across the dangerous neck of snow to rejoin Culbert on the snow plateau. He left the rope behind in the crevasse. Culbert had started to pull it through, but it had got stuck somewhere. He could not go back into the crevasse without a belay, so they would return for it the following day.

From the point where he had fallen, right back to the plateau, the overhanging cornice had been cut back and trimmed like a hedge by the swinging rope, so that he could see exactly what line to take. And by the time he had covered the first fifty feet, Culbert had thrown a rope down to him, and he moved confidently on up to the plateau. It was almost dark now, and there was no sign of anyone from below. They needn't have stirred from the tent.

Culbert grinned down at him affectionately. 'Nice to see you, you old bugger.' Emery gave a sheepish grin. 'Thanks, you old bastard.' Two and a half hours of tension was completely relieved, and they roared with laughter.

Next day the weather was not quite so bad, and by late afternoon it was showing definite signs of improvement. The following morning, 13 September, began mistily, but it soon began to clear, and at midday they decided that it was worth trying to push on.

Camp IV was on a sort of shelf about a thousand feet below the crest of the north-east ridge and probably not more than a few hours' climb from it once the route was made. Above Camp IV, the ground rose quickly and steeply in the form of a ridge which slanted up from right to left. To get on to this ridge they had to cross a snow bridge over a huge crevasse which lay right across their path. To the left of the snow bridge the far wall of the crevasse faced them like a rampart; and at the top of this far wall was the slanting ridge. As they climbed up this ridge they would have to keep a little to the right of the crest, which on this side fell straight into the crevasse. The drop into the crevasse itself would be a fall of two to three hundred feet, and the crevasse opened out on to the flank of the mountain, giving a clear drop of several thousand feet into the Stak Valley. It was a line to keep well back from.

Several times in the previous week they had tried to force their way up towards the snow bridge and left on to the ridge, but each time they had been driven back by waist-deep snow. The condition of the snow was still bad and it was extremely hard work forcing their way through, but as long as the weather held good, the snow surface would slowly improve, and it was nothing like so dangerous now that the mist had cleared and visibility was good. They crossed the crevasse, turned left and started up the ridge. Their track was now pointing almost directly up towards the complex of peaks that formed Haramosh II, still hidden by the many humps and pinnacles ahead. To their right lay the north-east ridge, again completely hidden by broken ground except for one striking snow formation exactly like a cardinal's hat, which dominated the whole area, and which must almost certainly be on the ridge itself. If they were unable to get through to Haramosh II, it looked as though they might be able to break out on to the ridge somewhere near the Cardinal's hat. From this point they would be able to look down into the trough separating the two main peaks and see almost as much as they would from Haramosh II.

They climbed up the short, steep section of the ridge, turned right at the top, and started along the crest of the slope. They went quite well at first, and then the crest seemed to be narrowing, so that it looked as though somewhere ahead of them it might sharpen to a point. A crevasse suddenly appeared right across their track. Neither of them had seen this sort of thing straight across the crest of a ridge before. The only way to get over was to employ the swimming technique used successfully by Emery in the crevasse two days earlier. They got across safely and continued along the narrowing crest. They couldn't see more than a few feet ahead as the crest was still climbing slightly. Culbert, coming through to take up the lead, began to dislike the route intensely. To their right there was a cornice curling over away from them, ahead it looked as though the crest might suddenly stall and fall away beneath them, and to their left the ground fell away sheer to the Stak Valley. It looked as though they might be on snow and ice which had caked up against the cornice to form a false shelf. Potentially it was a very dangerous place indeed. After a discussion they retraced their steps, crossed the crevasse that bisected the crest of the ridge, and then turned left across the snow slope well down from the crest, in the direction of the Cardinal's hat. When they were about halfway across this snow slope they climbed up to a point just below the crevasse which had bisected the crest, and which ran along just below the top of this slope. They could now look back to Camp IV, and beyond Camp IV to the narrow neck of snow and the ice cliffs at the top of the slope leading down to the Haramosh glacier. They could see right down to the glacier itself, and to the long slope down from Camp III to the top of the icefall. In the clear, rarefied air they could see an unmistakable line in the snow, and where the line finished, three figures, ploughing their way through the waist-deep snow. There could have been no more comforting sight than that of their comrades, struggling in much the same way as they were, on their way up to join them.

They continued along the lower lip of the crevasse, eventually reaching a point where a short distance ahead of them they could see a large snow bridge crossing it. They still had a long way to go to the north-east ridge, but they could see the route ahead clearly. There was a lot of broken and crevassed ground between them and the north-east ridge, and the last part of the route steepened and was topped by ice cliffs, but another two days like today and they would reach the ridge. It was now late afternoon, and they returned to Camp IV. They had given themselves a good start for the following day, and at last it looked as though the break had come.

It was another clear day next day and they were quickly able to reach the point where they had stopped the previous evening. There had been very little snow in the night and the track was clear. But when they began to break fresh ground they again found themselves struggling through waist-deep snow, over rather broken ground which was still climbing gradually. The Cardinal's hat still rose up ahead of them to pinpoint their goal and dominate their thoughts. They stopped for a lunch of sardines and biscuits in the early afternoon, and as they sat on their rucksacks they gazed greedily at the incredible view. Never before had they reached this height; and never before had they been able to see the vast range of peaks to the east and south-east. Here it was that K2, the savage mountain, lifted its head triumphantly above its fellows, a giant molar pulled from the serrated teeth of the Himalaya.

They began climbing again, fairly gradually and with the condition of the snow improving steadily under the influence of two to three days' good weather, but making frequent detours to avoid crevasses. They could now see clearly the point at which they wanted to break out on to the ridge, just to the right of the Cardinal's hat, but to reach this point they would have to make a wide detour to the left to avoid a patch of very crevassed ground. They began this detour, climbing gradually all the time, finding the snow harder work again and their progress getting slower. The sun disappeared over the ridge ahead of them and the air was chill, but the effort of the climb kept them warm. It was five o'clock when they decided it was time to return to Camp IV. There was not a great deal of ground now between them and the north-east ridge.

The cold began to attack them directly they stopped climbing, and they put on their duvet suits before retracing their steps. The light was failing as they covered the last few hundred feet down to Camp IV, but down in the hollow they could see two figures busily erecting a tent. Streather and Jillott had fought their way up.

The two parties hadn't met for eight days and it was a pleasant reunion. Hamilton had accompanied Streather and Jillott up to Camp IV, but had gone back to Camp III before the others returned from the day's climb. Streather and Jillott had watched him all the way down to Camp III, which he was to keep open for their return in a day or so. There was a great deal to talk about. Streather suggested that they should pair off differently in the two tents, Culbert joining him while Jillott went in with Emery, and it worked well. Jillott told Emery of their difficulties in finding the route through the icefall and of the digging of the snow cave, while Emery related the crevasse incident and full details of the work they had put in on the route up towards the north-east ridge. They could hear snatches of conversation and laughter coming from the other tent, and knew that much the same thing was happening there.

9

THE AVALANCHE

There was a good deal of mist and cloud about early next morning, but this quickly gave way to sunshine and the promise of a fine day. Soon it settled down into one of the best days they'd had, not unlike a bright spring day in England. The weather added the final touch to their buoyant anticipation, so that they had breakfast, packed their rucksacks and recharged their cameras in light-hearted mood.

Even so, the various tasks they had to do still took a long time, and it was eleven o'clock before they began to move off along the lip of the crevasse above Camp IV. Culbert and Jillott led the way along the well-established track, with Emery and Streather following. There had been very little snow during the night, the old snow in the track had frozen hard, and the going was easy. They crossed the big snow bridge over the crevasse, Jillott leading, with Culbert pausing to look back towards K2 and take a few camera shots. Streather and Emery, too, gazed for a long time at the vast triangle of K2. It was a poignant moment for Streather, and memories of the epic struggle on that mountain with the Americans four years earlier crowded into his mind. There were years when almost any great mountain could be impossible to climb. It had been such a year for them on K2; yet the following year the Italians had climbed it. It was such a year for them on Haramosh.

Eventually they reached the highest point reached by Culbert and Emery the previous day, and here they shed their rucksacks and sat down on them to have lunch. They enjoyed a pleasant and leisurely meal of biscuits, sweets and water mixed with lemonade crystals, and discussed the route ahead and the point they ought to aim at to break out on to the north-east ridge. From now on they had to make the track, and the real work of the day started.

Between them and the line of the ridge they would have to move up over rather steeper ground, over a crevasse and between some ice cliffs. They couldn't see exactly what lay between the ice cliffs and the ridge, but this was the obvious way to start. However, three days of good weather had packed the snow down a lot and the surface was improving all the time. The loose snow was only thigh-deep now and they moved through it steadily.

Jillott led at first, crossing the crevasse and moving up the slope towards the ice cliffs, where Culbert took over. The ground became really steep now. Finally Streather and Emery came through and took over the lead on the last stretch from the top of the ice cliffs up towards the ridge. They could see that just short of the ridge was a huge crevasse, and beyond this the last steep slope up to the crest of the ridge. The crest itself curled over towards them in an impressive cornice which was quite small at the point they were making for, but which only a few yards higher up the ridge became very large indeed, culminating in the great Cardinal's hat formation which dominated the whole area. Even at the point they had chosen they would have to work hard to get through it.

But for the moment the crevasse itself looked the bigger problem. It didn't open up directly beneath them, but sloped down diagonally away from them into the mountain, so that the whole of the far lip was one complete overhang. They couldn't be sure how far on to the upper lip they would have to get before they reached safe ground. Eventually they decided on a plan. Streather and Emery stood together on the lower lip, belayed from behind by Jillott and Culbert. Streather stuck his ice axe into the upper lip directly opposite and almost at the same level. Emery leaned forward and swung his axe as high up on the far lip as he could. He then stepped on to Streather's axe and hauled up on his own as quickly as he could, sped by a shove from behind by Streather. Streather then followed the same route, with no one to shove from behind but with the great advantage of having Emery above him to haul on the rope. Now they took a firm belay on the upper lip and hauled first Culbert and then Jillott across. By the time it came to Jillott's turn, with three of them hauling on the rope, he literally shot across.

Twenty feet above them was the cornice. They were sure that they had reached the north-east ridge at last and were on the last part of it leading up to Haramosh II. Even so, it was possible that they might be mistaken. This might be a false crest. Beyond it they might find further difficulties, insuperable difficulties, separating them from the view they had come to see.

Streather led the way up the last twenty feet, belayed from below, and began cutting his way through the cornice. The loose powdery snow covered him up to the hips and broke off down the slope to cover the boots of the others. He kept his eyes on his axe as he thrust it this way and that, opening up a gap of about five feet. Bit by bit the cornice came away. He climbed through the gap and lifted his head.

He was not a demonstrative man, but what he saw made him give an involuntary shout, a gasp, a bellow of shock and delight and amazement. All that they had struggled and yearned to see lay there before them but in a form and on a scale which was flabbergasting, which ridiculed their puny imaginations and made the realisation of the dream almost intolerably satisfying. He shouted down to the others. 'Come on up! You can't imagine what you'll see when you get here.'

They joined him on the far side of the cornice. Straight ahead, about three miles distant, rose the final peak of Haramosh, superb in its isolation, dominating the rest of the mountain like a citadel. Immediately in front of them the flank of the north-east ridge fell away down a convex slope so severe that only the first forty feet or so was visible from the ridge. Between them and the main summit lay the long trough, the first part invisible because of the convex slope. This trough now revealed itself as being not a smoothly curved bed of snow stretched out between the two peaks but a vast glacier fed by the final shoulder and cone of Haramosh itself, horribly crevassed and broken and littered with rock abutments and icefalls, a mass of ice cliffs and minor snow summits. Now their eyes followed the curve of the north-east ridge as it carried away to the left in a wide semicircle, rising to the complex of Haramosh II about a third of the way round and then sagging in the middle before climbing the last mile or so to the main summit.

But perhaps most impressive of all was the view to the north down into the Kutwal Valley, nearly 10,000 feet below. They had the most wonderful view of the valley and the Mani glacier, and could pick out every feature of the valley – the lake, the thin line of pine trees on the ridge of the lateral moraine, the straggling village, the forest of silver birch, the green pastures of the lower mountain slopes. Yet how small it all looked! It was as though down there they had been children, feeling a child's illusion of spaciousness in a suburban back garden.

Now they could see how the mountain hugged this great trough of snow and ice to its bosom, acquisitively, but unable to hold it all, spilling it regularly over the north face in the form of avalanches, leaking it down the mountainside in great hanging glaciers, dribbling it down to the valley in a myriad snow gullies. Here before them lay the secrets of Haramosh, the womb which gave birth to teeming life on the hot dusty plains many thousands of feet below and hundreds of miles distant. The four men gazed spellbound, and none of them spoke for a long time.

Eventually they moved down ten feet or so from the cornice and chose a safe place to sit down, before the slope steepened too severely. Streather turned to Jillott. 'Well, Bernard, what do you think?'

'I can't see much chance along there.'

Inevitably they felt a deep satisfaction at the complexity of the route ahead. It would have been too galling to have reached this point with such difficulty, only to find an easy route ahead which another week of fine weather would have enabled them to cover. Their reaction to the trough, with its inaccessible snow basin directly below them and the jagged glacier beyond, and the semicircle of the ridge, with its broken and switchback formation, was one of relief. It was wonderful to have reached this point, to have discovered the mountain's secrets and seen what no man had seen before them, but thank God there wasn't a route.

A stronger party, of course, given good weather and plenty of time, might make something of it. But for them there was no chance at all. They sat on their rucksacks for fully half an hour, taking in every feature that lay before them, still trying to imagine a possible route by means of the north-east ridge, appraising and evaluating, studying the final cone, which would be shrouded in cloud for a time and then appear again triumphantly, tantalisingly clear. Even supposing they had been able to traverse round the ridge, that final pyramid might have defeated them. It rose 3,000 feet above the ridge, the first two-thirds of which was a tremendous snow shoulder formidably steep, heavily crevassed and skirted by ice cliffs. It looked the sort of climb which would provide a difficult problem in the Alps; and while there was probably no reason why they shouldn't climb it at this altitude, they would need good supplies and plenty of time. And even then there remained the final cone. What had looked little more than a pimple from below now seemed almost a mountain in itself, a precipitous rock tower covered with ice.

The cloud was building up in the basin below them and around the main summit. None of them cared to think about the time. This was their last day, and they would prolong this moment as long as possible. It had a sweetness and a satisfaction that stemmed partly from the realisation of achievement and partly from the disappointments and frustrations that had gone before. They had completed their reconnaissance, and only just in time.

Many times during the past few weeks each member of the party had asked himself whether the expedition had been worthwhile. Now they had their answer. It was worth coming all this way and enduring all the discomforts and privations for this view alone. And there were many, many other compensations. They sat there chewing chocolate, relaxed and happy, all their difficulties forgotten, laughing at former strains, a team as never before. For some weeks now, these men had been shedding something of their individualism, pooling their resources, drawing strength from each other, becoming a team. Each man had contributed to it in his own way; for some it had been easier than for others. Throughout August they had each kept a personal diary. But in the first few days of September, one by one they had stopped writing, all within two or three days of each other. It was as though they could no longer keep secrets, no longer express themselves except together.

They began to talk about going back. But first, Jillott wanted to climb a little way along the ridge to the top of the Cardinal's hat that had stood out so clearly on the way up. It was an obvious vantage point and from it he thought he might get an even more dramatic view of the trough and the valley.

'Will you come up with me, John?' he called to Emery. 'Then Tony can take a picture of us. It's as near the top of the mountain as we'll get.'

Emery roped up with Jillott, and the two men prepared to move off. It was in keeping with their mood of elation that they should want to reach just one more dominant point before going down.

'Keep well back from the cornice,' shouted Streather. 'It's one of the biggest cornices I've seen.'

'We'll keep well down,' said Jillott.

'I'll sing out if it looks as though you're getting too close.'

'Right.'

The pinnacle was only about a hundred feet distant, and being right on the crest of the ridge, the slope up to it was easy. Jillott and Emery moved quickly across a small crevasse and up towards the pinnacle. Some forty feet from the top, and well down the slope, Emery stopped to take a belay and Jillott began to cover the last few yards to the pinnacle. Both men had kept so well clear of the cornice that Streather, watching anxiously, had not needed to shout a warning. He had taken several photographs and was preparing to take a last shot as soon as Jillott reached the pinnacle and turned to look down. Emery was taking a particularly firm belay with the cornice in mind, and Jillott had covered the last few yards to the pinnacle and had almost reached the point at which he was going to stop, when there was a muffled explosion which seemed to come from under their feet, followed by a crunching, tearing sound, and almost simultaneously the snow on which Jillott and Emery were standing began to move.

For a fraction of a second it seemed to Streather and Culbert that the other two climbers were simply playing about. Their first reaction was to laugh at the comical way in which they were throwing their arms and legs about, jerkily, like puppets, their weight not properly planted on the ground. But in the same instant they understood the awful significance of the muffled explosion, the tearing sound, and the telltale crack in the snow a few feet above Jillott. They stood like statues, dumbfounded, fearful to move lest the avalanche spread, horrified by the ghastly sight of their two comrades being swept helplessly past them with sudden and terrifying acceleration, down the convex slope and away out of sight.

The snow basin immediately below them was hidden by the curve of the slope, so that they could not see where Jillott and Emery fell. And the avalanche had thrown up clouds of snow which reduced the visibility in its path to nil. But they could still see down into the trough, half a mile distant and a thousand feet below. Here in a few moments the billowing clouds of snow crept forward, more slowly now because of the distance, like steam exhaled from a train. Streather and Culbert stood transfixed as the avalanche surged on with the weight and power of a great surf-breaker, smashing on to the rocky ice cliffs at the edge of the trough in a storm of snow spray, and plunging at last with mighty release over the north face.

These were the great avalanches that they had seen from the valley, crashing down the north face on to the glacier. They had never dreamt that one such avalanche might carry two of their comrades with it.

It had all happened with such stupefying suddenness, their situation had changed so abruptly from contentment to disaster, that it was impossible for them to take it in. Eventually Streather moved across to the point of the avalanche, where the surface was now firm and denuded of all excess snow, belayed by Culbert. From here he was able to look down the slope into the snow basin below. Flurries of powder snow were still settling, but as he looked he thought he detected movement. Then, to his astonishment and joy, he saw a figure moving about in the snow. There was no mistaking that green windproof suit. It was Jillott.

He watched incredulously as Jillott seemed to bend over and dig his hands in the snow. Soon, like a chicken hatching from an egg, another figure broke out of the snow. It was Emery, apparently buried by the avalanche. Both men stood up and seemed to shake themselves. Streather expressed his incredulous relief by shouting again and again across to Culbert. By some miracle both climbers had survived the fall.

10

THE SNOW BASIN

All four climbers had been so obsessed with the danger from the cornice that the thought of the slope avalanching had not occurred to them. Indeed at this point the slope didn't seem steep enough to avalanche. Streather had watched continually for signs of avalanche conditions; and although he had realised that this north-east ridge, falling away as abruptly as it did at this point into the snow basin, was not a particularly healthy spot, to anyone keeping back from the point where the slope steepened, and keeping down from the cornice, it had looked perfectly safe. But the truth was that this was the first time they had stood on a slope facing north-west. The action of wind and weather was different in each quarter, and it was evident from the height of the cornice and the avalanche itself that a great weight of snow was thrown against this slope in spells of bad weather.

For Jillott and Emery the moment of the avalanche, a fraction of a second in time, had been split into three distinct parts: perplexity, alarm, resignation. There was no question of their being able to jump clear or get out of the way; the whole sloping surface moved with them, a stretch of snow the size of a large room. It was as though they were standing on an enormous angled plate, stable enough in itself but connected to nothing, anchored to nothing. They barely had time to register the fact that they were being avalanched before they were involved in it; no time to think what they might do beyond the realisation that they could do nothing.

They knew that they were falling down the steep convex slope into the snow basin at the start of the trough, and they guessed that this might involve a fall of a thousand feet or so. The start of the snow basin had been invisible from the ridge, and they had little idea what they might be falling into. But as soon as the fall began, it seemed that by a selective shutdown of the senses, their bodies assumed a sort of protective cocoon. This impression was magnified by the cotton-wool protection of the snow that was falling with them. They weren't really aware of any reaction, and yet it seemed that automatically they were doing the things they had been trained to do in these circumstances – trying to hold on to their ice axes, and trying to dig in with them to hold the fall. At the same time they were aware that these things made absolutely no difference, that they were still falling and that the whole of their immediate world was falling with them.

They knew at first that they were falling down a very steep slope; and then they were suddenly conscious that they were hurtling through space. This seemed to go on for a long time – for several hundred feet. Then they were subconsciously aware of a considerable shock; they registered the fact of shock, but their bodies didn't really feel anything. Then they seemed to continue falling, rolling, down a shallower slope, until at last they came to a stop. And as soon as they stopped, the shutdown of the senses ceased, not immediately, but gradually, like coming round after an anaesthetic. It was several seconds before the restored control over body and limb registered in the brain.

To Emery it seemed that this restoration of consciousness only aggravated his difficulties. He seemed to be stuck in one position as in a dream, an odd position which he was unable to do anything to change. His legs were at a grotesque angle, his left hip was hurting, and he couldn't move at all. He was aware that Jillott was calling to him; he tried to sit up, but collapsed again into the snow.

'I can't move, Bernard.'

'You must, you must.' Jillott came over to him and took hold of his leg, trying to straighten it. Emery shouted with the pain, and Jillott let go. Eventually Emery managed to struggle into a kneeling position, his left leg still dragging grotesquely. He realised that he had dislocated his hip: the ball had jumped right out of its socket. In this state he would be a complete passenger.

And in the fall they had suffered another and even more serious misfortune. They had both lost their ice axes. They had survived the fall, but only now were they beginning to realise the extent of the catastrophe. Looking up they saw a line of ice cliffs perhaps 200 feet above them and at least 300 feet in depth, over which they must have fallen. This explained the sensation of falling through space, and the bump at the bottom. Above the ice cliffs was the steep snow slope, rising almost as sheer as the cliffs. The cliffs themselves looked impenetrable, and without ice axes they would never be able to ascend that slope. Between them and the ice cliffs was the shallower slope of the basin down which they had rolled at the end of the fall; but at the top of this slope, just below the ice cliffs, was a bergschrund, or huge crevasse. Fortunately they had overshot it in the fall, but it would be extremely dangerous and perhaps impossible to cross it again without ice axes for a belay. There was no other way out of the snow basin except over the ice cliffs at the top of the north face, and that would be a route of despair. Even so, both climbers had in mind that if they were unable to get out in any other way, and the others couldn't get down to them, they would virtually throw themselves over that precipitous north face and see what happened to them. It would be a million to one chance against reaching the glacier safely, but they would take that chance rather than sit here and die of exposure.

After a few minutes Emery turned to look again up the slope in an involuntary movement, and quite fortuitously he happened to turn the right way and the ball of his hip jumped back into its socket. It must have been resting right on the lip. He stood firmly on both feet for the first time since the fall. His hip still felt rickety and uncertain, but it was working.

Emery had lost two pairs of gloves in the fall; Jillott had lost the gloves from one hand. This might be very serious if they were forced to spend the night in the open, as it seemed that they certainly would be. It was now early evening, and there couldn't be much daylight left. They knew that Streather and Culbert would be trying to get down to them, and they knew, too, that they must try and help themselves. Jillott picked up Emery's red and white ski cap and stuck it on his head, and they started to move off up the slope, rather shakily, but still roped together. They were ready for action, but without ice axes they felt confused and disorganised, like a riderless horse.

Straight ahead the ice cliffs were sheer and impenetrable, and to the left they looked almost equally difficult. The only possible plan seemed to be to traverse across the slope to the right, where the cliffs eventually seemed to peter out. But immediately below the cliffs was the bergschrund, separating the snow basin from the ice cliffs, and this extended across the whole slope. The immediate problem was going to be to cross the bergschrund.

They began to make their way across the lower slope to the right, towards the point where the ice cliffs petered out. Emery's ski cap was dribbling half-melted snow down his neck and he pulled it off and dropped it. They went on slowly. But when they reached the lower lip of the crevasse, just below the point at which the cliffs petered out, they found that they couldn't possibly get across at this point. It gaped widely, the upper lip looked rotten, and while it might have been worth trying with ice axes it was quite unjustifiable without. So they continued traversing across the slope to the right, following along the lower lip of the crevasse, until they reached a point at which they could cross fairly safely. They both got across, but now they found they were cut off and unable to work their way back along the upper lip of the crevasse. So they started up the slope straight ahead.

About ten feet up the slope they came to bare ice. It was quite impossible to kick steps in this effectively, but they went on trying. Almost at once, both men slipped and came off simultaneously, falling down towards the crevasse. Jillott cleared the crevasse completely and rolled on down the slope of the basin, while Emery fell right across the lower lip and lay suspended over the edge. It was an uncomfortable moment, but it saved him from rolling down the slope.

It was clear that they weren't going to be able to get out like this, and they had no other ideas. It was now dusk, and there was no point in trying to do any more for the time being. The best plan seemed to be to traverse back across the slope to a point roughly below the ice cliffs where they had originally fallen, in the track of the avalanche, and stamp out a platform. Then if the others were cutting their way down they would find them.

They kicked out their platform, unroped and sat down. It was almost dark. Emery unzipped the fly of his windproof trousers and stuck his hands in his crutch. Jillott sat beside him, keeping his hands warm in the same way. They waited for the night hours to pass.

Emery got up and stamped around every few minutes; and a mild attack of dysentery, which he had been suffering from for some days, troubled him several times. Jillott was feeling the cold even more. He huddled close to Emery; but, protecting their hands as they were, they were unable to hold on to each other, and it was a cheerless business. Both men had spent a night out on a mountain before, and although it hadn't been at anywhere near this height, they knew what to expect. If you were engaged on a certain standard of climb, under certain conditions, almost inevitably at some time in your career you'd be forced to bivouac for the night. It wasn't the sort of thing you went out of your way to do, but it was the sort of thing that most climbers gave some thought to, wondering what it would be like. Emery, in fact, had quite looked forward to his first experience, which had enabled him to test a theory. He had imagined that in such a situation it might be possible to diminish the extreme physical discomfort by a sort of mental trick. You might be able to shut out the physical discomfort by taking refuge in the mind. However, an experience in the Alps had taught him that this just wasn't possible. You were too tired, too wet, too hungry, and above all too cold, to make the mind work on that level at all. All that happened was that you got some snatch of song running through your head, or you perhaps thought of people, but you couldn't for any appreciable time shut off the physical side of things. It was too unpleasant.

Still, the fact that they knew what to expect was some help. They knew that the night was going to pass slowly, and they were prepared for it.

In spite of the obvious difficulties, neither Jillott nor Emery had any real doubt that the others would get down to them. And about halfway through the night they saw a light, high above them on the upper slope. They called out several times, but could hear no answering shout. Nevertheless, to two men in their desperate plight, knowing as they did that they couldn't possibly survive more than two or three nights at this altitude without food or drink or shelter, and seeing little hope of getting out by themselves, the light was enormously encouraging.

'Do you think we should try and work our way up towards them?' asked Emery.

'Yes, I think we should.'

They knew now that they couldn't get up the slope to their right, so they began to move off towards the left. Even if they couldn't get beyond the ice cliffs, or even beyond the bergschrund, they would be at the nearest point to the others in readiness for dawn.

They started to move across the slope, still unroped, Emery leading, and they had gone no more than four or five paces when Emery fell over an ice cliff which he hadn't seen in the dark. Fortunately it was only about twenty feet high and he didn't hurt himself, but it was enough to show them the futility of attempting to move before dawn. He was able to direct Jillott round the ice cliff and down, and they stamped out another platform and spent the rest of the night there. They didn't see the light again, and they wondered if perhaps they had imagined it. There had been no answering shouts. They slept fitfully, awakened by bad dreams. Sometimes, in a half-conscious state, they thought they saw the light again, and they shouted. It seemed a long time till dawn.

◇◇◇◇◇◇

For Streather and Culbert, the relief and delight at seeing that their comrades had survived the avalanche was soon tempered by the full realisation of the perilous situation they were in. They were both almost certainly suffering from injuries sustained in the fall. Already it was late afternoon and there was little hope of getting down to them that night. Indeed it seemed that there was very little hope of getting them out of the snow basin at all. It was a most inaccessible spot; and a slope that had avalanched once might avalanche again. It occurred to Streather, in a moment of hard realism, that it might have been better for Jillott and Emery had they been killed in the fall. They were trapped in the snow basin, and there they might all too easily stay.

'I can't see how we're going to get them out,' he told Culbert. 'I can't see how we'll get down to them. This slope's terribly steep and it's in a treacherous state. They're almost certain to be hurt. I can't see how we'll do it.'

Culbert was completely unruffled. 'Don't worry, Tony. We'll get down to them.'

Anxious though he still felt, Streather found Culbert's confidence immensely reassuring. Certainly if it was humanly possible they would get them out. He began to work out what was the best thing to do. Jillott and Emery both had good heads. They would be all right tonight.

The wisest thing was for Culbert and himself to go back to Camp IV, get plenty of food and drink and at least a little rest, and then start out at dawn, carrying more food and drink for Jillott and Emery and as much rope as they could find. Having decided this, it remained to try and get some warm clothes and food down to them tonight.

Streather and Culbert took off their eiderdown coats and put them in one of the rucksacks, together with some spare gloves and scarves, a bottle of water, and some sweets and chocolate. Streather addressed a note to them on an empty packet of film, saying 'Try to keep warm; we'll get down to you as soon as we can.' Streather moved once again to the point where the avalanche had started, belayed by Culbert, and dropped the rucksack down the slope. At first they lost sight of it as it reached the steepest part of the slope, but when it reappeared down in the basin they could see that it was running well wide of Jillott and Emery. They watched in dismay as it spiralled and cavorted away to the right, disappearing at length into a crevasse which opened on to the north face.

'We'd better get back to Camp IV as quickly as we can,' said Streather. 'Perhaps we can start down to them tonight.'

'Do you think they'll be trying to get up?' asked Culbert.

'Now that they haven't got our note, or the clothing and food, I think they probably will. There'll be a moon later. We may be able to get down to them tonight.'

They hurried back to Camp IV in failing light. The trudge up to the ridge had taken them four hours earlier in the day, but they covered the distance back in just over an hour. Whatever else they did they must eat well themselves for all their sakes, and they spent some time in cooking a meal. Then they looked around for odd articles of clothing. Culbert found an extra shirt and Streather found a thin jersey – poor substitutes for their lost eiderdown jackets, but better than nothing. They made two Thermos flasks of soup to take back to Jillott and Emery, found another 200 feet of rope, and then set out for the ridge.

It was ten o'clock when they reached it. The moon was up, but it was completely obscured by cloud, and the sky was darkened. Both men had torches. Streather stood for a moment at the top of the slope, deciding what to do. He could see absolutely nothing of the path ahead, due to the convex nature of the slope. Under normal conditions it was a route that he would have avoided at all costs. The slope was dangerously steep and the threat of avalanches remained. The safest way might be to start down on 300 feet of rope, with Culbert belaying him from the top. He would be able to get some idea of what lay lower down the slope, and of how they might work their way down to the others. Culbert could keep him on a fairly tight rope and if he slipped would be able to hold him.

He began to move off down the slope, his torch held in front of him. Culbert paid out the rope. The snow was soft at first, but suddenly it hardened. He must be in the track of the avalanche. This was much safer as the same area wouldn't avalanche again.

The slope steepened abruptly as he passed over the convex curve and out of sight of Culbert. He could no longer walk forwards. He had to turn and face the slope, reaching down with first one leg and then the other, like going backwards down a ladder. He kicked each step carefully, plunging his ice axe into the snow at his ankles and then reaching down with his foot. Every few moments he half turned and shone his torch down the slope, shouting as he did so. Soon he heard answering shouts.

He made his way more quickly now, guided and encouraged by the shouts from below. Then the rope seemed to be pulling and he gave it a tug. He shouted up the slope to Culbert, but could hear no reply.

He realised that he must have come down the full 300 feet of rope and that it was now pulling taut. There was no change in the slope, no feature which suggested any relief from this almost sheer climb down to the basin. It was easy to overestimate the angle of a slope, but he'd never climbed on a slope steeper than this. It must be fully sixty degrees. Standing as he was, stomach pressed hard into the snow, peering up into the darkness, it looked vertical.

He shouted to Culbert to start climbing down to him. There was still no reply. There was nothing for it but to climb all the way back up the slope.

The steps he had made were good, and his feet and hands found them unerringly. He moved with a slow steady rhythm, as unhurried as ever. If you had to spend a night out on a mountain, climbing was the best way to keep warm.

As he neared the top he shouted again to Culbert, and was relieved to hear him answer this time. His earlier shouts must have been cut off by the hump in the slope. Culbert hauled on the rope and helped him up the last hundred feet.

Streather decided that 300 feet of rope was only a hazard since it wouldn't reach all the way, and that a normal length of rope of about a hundred feet would be best. They untied the rope and started down, belaying each other every hundred feet. Soon they reached the point where Streather had been forced to stop. They were still climbing down backwards, Streather leading, moving with extreme care on the hard-packed surface, still in the track of the avalanche. It was tedious work and they lost all count of time. Occasionally they shone their torches down the slope, and the shouts from below seemed to get closer. They were astonished when it began to get light.

Even now, because of the curve of the slope, they couldn't see what lay immediately below them. But they could see Jillott and Emery now, standing up and waving to them, apparently unhurt. They could hear them shouting, but all they could make out was something about moving over to the right. Streather seemed to be directly above them and he was sure he was in the right position, so he kept going straight down. Then, as he half turned to make sure he was keeping in a straight line, he saw a line of ice cliffs below him to the left. Evidently these cliffs ran right underneath them and this was why the others had been shouting at them to change direction.

He kept on until he judged he was about ten feet above the ice cliffs. There seemed to be no way down, and the others were still pointing across to their right – to his own right as well, as he came backwards down the slope. They would have to traverse along the top of the ice cliffs until they came to a point where they could get down. Evidently there was such a point further along.

Streather looked along the line of the traverse. The slope was still extremely steep, and cutting a line directly across it would be a difficult and arduous task. So far they had been able to keep in the track of the avalanche, but across the traverse they would move out of this line. There was no saying in what condition the snow surface might be.

11
THE TREACHEROUS TRAVERSE

Jillott and Emery watched anxiously as Streather and Culbert began on the traverse. With any luck the others would join them in another two or three hours; and they began moving across to a position just below the crevasse, opposite the point where the ice cliffs gave out. But as they watched, it became apparent that the surface on which the others were moving had changed.

Streather and Culbert seemed to have come almost completely to a stop. They didn't seem to be making any progress at all. Jillott and Emery watched them cutting a way along the top of the ice cliffs, moving painfully slowly. The surface must be hard ice, desperately hard ice. They ran their eyes along the top of the cliffs to the point where the cliffs gave out and the slope plunged on down to the bergschrund. At their present rate they would be many, many hours on the traverse, probably all day.

Jillott and Emery completed their move across to the point at which the cliffs petered out and stood just short of the lower lip of the bergschrund. Ahead of them the slope still looked terribly steep. Even when Streather and Culbert had finished the traverse they had a very nasty climb of about 300 feet down to the snow basin to meet them.

Fortunately, providentially, the weather was holding good. There would be no chance for any of them if the weather changed now.

It was warm in the sun and Jillott and Emery felt their bodies slowly thawing out from the night in the basin. They felt drowsy and languid. There was nothing they could do but sit there and watch the others moving step by step across the slope towards them. It was horribly frustrating. They were still suffering from the effects of the fall, and the lack of food and drink was beginning to tell. They sat in a half stupor, unable to think much for themselves, conscious of their complete dependence on those two slowly moving figures silhouetted against the white slope. They were conscious, too, of the colossal feat of endurance that was being enacted up there: Streather and Culbert must have been climbing almost continuously since eleven o'clock yesterday.

◇◇◇◇◇◇

Throughout the day Streather and Culbert took it in turns to lead. The ice was as hard as concrete; chipping at it hardly did more than splinter the surface – they had to hack at it with all their strength. Cutting steps across a steep ice-slope was one of the most awkward of all climbing movements. You could bring your outside leg forward fairly readily, although it was very difficult to keep in a straight line. But bringing your inside leg through, the leg against the slope, balancing your weight on it tentatively, and planting it firmly in front of you in a step you'd cut with great difficulty, was an almost unbearable strain on the muscles, besides being extremely precarious. Exhausted as they were from the night's climb, this traverse seemed brutally long. The whole body from the waist down, and indeed even the shoulders and neck, had to be held in a twisted and deformed position for hour after hour, when the instinct of every muscle was to relax and give in.

It was late afternoon before they realised that they were nearing the end of the traverse. They could see the others quite clearly now, huddled together beyond the bergschrund. Streather and Culbert hailed them again and again, and they answered, but neither could make out what the others were saying.

'Start climbing up the slope,' called Streather. 'Start climbing.' And then when his words seemed to have no effect: 'Start climbing, however difficult it is. It's a matter of life and death.'

'We can't cross the crevasse,' Jillott and Emery shouted. 'We've lost our ice axes.' But Streather and Culbert couldn't hear.

They had almost reached the end of the ice cliff now, and the slope was beginning to fall away down to the bergschrund. On the traverse the slope had eased to fifty-five degrees; but here it steepened to sixty as it plunged down the last 300 feet to the basin. For a moment, as the ice cliff petered out, it seemed to be even steeper, so that they had to carry on with the traverse, finding it impossible to start cutting their way down and losing height.

Reaching down with their ice axes to cut steps down this last slope would be the hardest thing of all. It was almost impossible to cut steps going down as steeply as this. You simply couldn't get any weight into your ice axe ahead of you down the slope without losing your balance.

Just before they left the traverse, Streather noticed a dark object in one of the steps that Culbert had just cut. It looked like a crampon – he was sure it was a crampon. He called to Culbert. 'Rae! Hold on. You've left a crampon in that last step.' Culbert, balancing on his right foot, bringing his left leg through against the slope and planting it in front of him, realised as he put it in the new step that something was wrong. He stopped, turned, and began the awkward business of moving a step back along the traverse to retrieve the crampon. As he moved, the climbing rope, dangling in the snow, caught the crampon and lifted it out of the step, sending it hurtling down the steepest part of the slope into the bergschrund. For a brief moment the two men, now facing one another, caught each other's eye. Both realised how serious the loss of a crampon at this stage might be.

Culbert tried to go on, but he had to let Streather take over, and he had to take his left canvas overboot off in order to gain any foothold at all with his climbing boot. Eventually they reached a point directly above where Jillott and Emery were sitting. Now they had to get safely down the steep slope to the bergschrund. Obviously it was going to be very nasty indeed. There was about a foot of snow covering the ice on the slope, much of the snow was rotten, and it was extremely difficult to get any sort of grip. Even so, the covering of snow meant that they were able to kick steps, which they had been unable to do on the traverse.

It was now late afternoon, the sun had gone down, and the cold of the evening was upon them. But the effect of this was to harden and bind the rotten snow on the slope and make the kicking of steps easier. Between them they kicked and cut a level platform in the slope where they finished the traverse, and Culbert stood on this platform and belayed Streather down. The method of descent was exactly the same as it had been on the upper slope – Streather went down backwards, kicking the steps beneath him, getting his foot firmly embedded in one step and then reaching down still further to kick a step with the other, his hands gripping the steps he had recently made. He felt like a spider crawling backwards down a wall, a thin strand of web stretched out above him in case he should fall.

When Streather reached the end of the climbing rope, Culbert came down in his steps and then passed him and began kicking and crawling down in the same way. Then, when the rope was exhausted again, Streather took over. It was extremely awkward to pass each other on the slope, but they managed it with care. At last they reached the bottom of the slope above the bergschrund. Here Streather advanced to the upper lip of the great crevasse and lowered a rope to Jillott and Emery. They tied on and crossed the crevasse one by one.

The reunion, a moment of great warmth, was strangely inarticulate. The gratitude felt by Jillott and Emery was mostly unspoken. What did one say to men who had climbed without pause day and night under the most treacherous and exhausting conditions, climbing all the time towards danger rather than away from it? There were words enough in the English language to fit such an occasion, but it wasn't like the English to use them. The most that Jillott and Emery could manage was a muttered 'Thanks, Tony' and 'Thanks, Rae.' Even that, charged with gratitude as it was, seemed almost too much.

Streather and Culbert, immensely relieved to find Jillott and Emery not seriously hurt and in good heart, gave them the two flasks of soup and some glucose tablets. Unfortunately one of the flasks had broken on the climb down the slope, and they were forced to pour the precious liquid, now thickened and rattling with silver glass, away. To Jillott and Emery the soup in the other flask seemed no more than a mouthful.

Although the light was already failing, none of them had any doubt that the right thing to do was to begin the climb out that night. They had no more food or liquid, the best way to keep warm was to keep moving, and they would gain absolutely nothing by spending the night in the basin and waiting for morning. Each man had already drawn heavily on his reserves of strength, but he was hardly likely to build them up again by snatching what rest he could in the open at this height.

As Jillott and Emery were without ice axes, Streather joined the two ropes together so that in effect they were all climbing on one rope. He was confident that now the steps were made they would all succeed in getting out of the basin, and he felt that being roped together would add to their sense of assurance and comradeship. It would take them some hours to get to the top, but it wouldn't be anything like the tedious and precarious business it had been coming down.

Culbert led the way up the lower slope, followed by Streather, then Jillott and Emery. They seemed to be making height quickly, and it wasn't long before they were looking down some 200 feet beneath them to the bergschrund. Another hundred feet and they would reach the platform at the beginning of the traverse. At this point there was a grunt from above and Culbert, who had been having considerable difficulty on only one crampon, slipped and fell down the slope on to Streather, knocking Streather off as well. The weight of these two falling together dislodged Jillott and Emery like ninepins, and all four climbers fell in a tangled mass down the slope and across the bergschrund back into the snow basin.

Streather called the names of the climbers and they all answered cheerfully. Fortunately they had fallen in soft snow, and somehow they had managed to avoid spiking each other with their crampons. Streather had lost his ice axe, but Culbert had retained his.

It was now nearly dark, but they knew there would be a moon later, and they decided to try again, this time with Streather leading, using Culbert's ice axe, followed by Emery, who had found reserves of energy from somewhere and was now climbing confidently, then Culbert, with Jillott last. This time they made slow progress; but in spite of the darkness Streather could see above them the platform that he and Culbert had stamped out earlier in the day. That was the first landmark, the end of the first lap, and he kept going steadily to reach it. Their method of progression now was for Streather to climb fifty feet or so, take a belay, and then help the others up one at a time until they were all standing in the steps immediately below him. This was reasonably foolproof provided no one fell off while Streather was moving; and there was no reason why anyone should do this unless he collapsed or fell asleep. They made steady progress, and they had nearly reached the platform when Streather, moving up alone, felt a sustained heavy pull on the rope. The shaft of his ice axe was dug into the slope just above him to assist his climb, and he tried to hold the weight on this. Suddenly the tug was too much, he lost his foothold, and found himself swinging in mid-air. Now he felt himself falling again; and all four men, hopelessly entangled, dropped the 250 feet down to the far side of the bergschrund again and into the snow basin. Jillott, utterly exhausted, had gone to sleep in his tracks and dragged them all off one by one.

Getting out of the snow basin in their present state was obviously going to be a very much more difficult proposition than any of them had imagined. They were all tired and dispirited, they had lost the last ice axe, and no one felt like attempting that slope again before daylight. Perhaps after all it might be best to try to get a few hours' sleep. If they huddled together in a crevasse, they would at least be protected from the biting wind.

They moved up to the bergschrund and found a point where there was a ledge in the crevasse and where both the crevasse edges had an overhang that would prevent snow falling in on them. They climbed down about ten feet into the crevasse and on to the ledge. At this depth they found the crevasse was almost full of frozen snow and ice, with only one small gap leading down into the crevasse proper. They were able to jam themselves between the crevasse walls, shoulders against the lower lip and feet against the upper, so that there was no danger of falling through the gap.

They huddled together in an attempt to keep warm. Culbert particularly was troubled by his left foot, which had not had sufficient protection against the intense cold since he had been forced to remove the canvas overboot and had become frostbitten. At Streather's suggestion, Culbert took off his climbing boot as well and pushed his foot under Streather's shirt against his stomach, where Streather nursed it. If they could get the foot warm, there was a good chance that the circulation would return. Streather and the American Pete Schoening had saved their feet in this way on K2.

Streather and Culbert, being without their duvet jackets, lay in the middle, with Jillott and Emery on the outside. Somehow they all managed to snatch a little sleep. But during the night they were awakened by several shouts from Jillott. 'Will you go and get my tent for me?' he was saying. 'Come on, chaps, stop fooling about.' His voice sounded perfectly natural, but there was a note of strain in it, and now and again he would groan as though in pain. Streather roused Emery. 'I brought some morphia and a syringe down with me, in case either of you were injured,' he said. 'It sounds as though Bernard may be in pain. Can you give him an injection?'

Emery took the phial of morphia and tried to cut the top off so as to draw up the fluid into the syringe, but his fingers were so numb that he could feel nothing. He had lost his gloves in the first fall; Streather and Culbert had brought some spare socks down with them and he had put a pair of these on his hands, but he had lost these as well in one of the later falls. His hands were in bad shape, probably frostbitten. He had to give the phial back to Streather, who was able to knock the top off and fill the syringe. Emery climbed over the others to Jillott, tugged at his clothes until he had freed a small patch of his buttock, and gave him a jab. Jillott, wondering what was going on, protested all the time. 'It'll be all right, Bernard,' coaxed Emery. 'Just lie still.' Almost immediately after the injection, Jillott quietened and fell into a deep sleep.

It was very cramped on the ledge, and comfort for one almost inevitably meant discomfort for another. They seemed to be stiff and sore all over. Sometimes gusts of powder snow blew in on to them, but although the cold was intense they were protected from the wind. Somehow the night passed.

As soon as it started to get light, Streather began to climb up out of the crevasse. 'I'm going down the slope to disentangle the rope and see if I can find either of the ice axes,' he told the others. 'Will you help Rae on with his boot, John? We'd better get started as soon as we can.'

Streather soon found the rope, which was very badly tangled from the second fall of the previous night; but he could see no sign of either of the missing ice axes. He looked up at the lower slope straight above him and then along the top of the ice cliff, as he worked on disentangling the rope. Being without an ice axe would add to their difficulties, but along the dangerous traverse the steps were already cut. He still had good hopes that they would all get out of the basin, but the two abortive attempts of last night were a warning of how difficult it was going to be. The night's rest very probably hadn't done them any real good, but it would have been bad psychology to keep on struggling hopelessly in the darkness. Now they knew what they were up against, and there would be a determination to succeed first time today.

He still felt fairly strong himself, but he knew that the others had been less fortunate. Culbert's loss of a crampon had been cruel luck; it had not only reduced his climbing efficiency but had resulted in frostbite in the affected foot. Jillott was very probably suffering from concussion, and was obviously in an exhausted state. Emery had been climbing strongly last night, but his hands were frostbitten. Their minds and bodies would hardly withstand another day's frustration on the slope and another night out in the basin.

Streather looked up at the slope again grimly. They had a fateful day's climbing ahead of them. At the top of the slope, a thousand feet up, lay safety; but there was little hope for anyone who didn't get out of the basin today.

He knew it would be up to him to get them out, and the responsibility drained him of concern about himself. Nevertheless the thought of Sue, and of his young son Charles, now six months old, was always in his mind, sustaining him; somehow he must keep going.

The sun was now up and the air was slightly warmer. The weather was still clear. In the crevasse, Emery was struggling with Culbert's boot. Culbert had three pairs of socks on, and his foot had swollen from frostbite. Emery kept trying to force the boot on, but it wouldn't go. He realised how painful it must be. Culbert, as ever, made not the slightest complaint. In the end Culbert had to take off two pairs of socks to get the boot on. Emery then climbed up to the lip of the crevasse and called down to Streather that the boot was on. Streather came across and joined them. They now began a search for the lost ice axes and gloves. They found nothing.

Jillott thought he could see an axe sticking out at the bottom of the ice cliff some 400 yards to the left, one of the two that he and Emery had lost two days earlier. He decided to try and get it. He thought, too, that he might find an easier way back on to the ridge that way. Culbert, hampered by having only one crampon, decided to try this route as well. Streather and Emery, convinced that the only likely route lay to the right, moved off in that direction.

'We'll start remaking the steps up here,' said Streather. 'Then we shan't be wasting time. If you find anything, give us a shout.' He and Emery crossed the bergschrund, which had been partly filled at this point with snow brought down by their falls the previous night, and began on the slope.

Jillott and Culbert traversed across the basin for some distance before crossing the bergschrund just below the point where they thought they could see the ice axe. As they came up under the ice cliff, Jillott was sure that he was right. Regaining his ice axe would be a great start to the day. He stooped to pick it up, only to find that it was nothing more than a broken, useless shaft sticking out of the snow.

They had come some distance to the left and there was still no sign of a break in the ice cliff. With an ice axe they might have explored a little further, but now it was pointless. They decided to retrace their steps and catch up with the others.

Streather and Emery seemed to be gaining height very slowly indeed. All the steps they had kicked so laboriously in this slope had been broken or wiped away in the previous night's falls. Now, with no ice axe, Streather began punching the hard snow with his clenched fists until he had enough depth for a purchase, pulling himself up, punching more cup-shaped holes, and then kicking the lower holes out into proper steps. At first he winced from the pain in his hands as he beat out the steps, but soon his knuckles went numb and he felt nothing. Emery behind him did the same, improving the steps all the way.

They looked down from time to time and watched Jillott and Culbert, first going away from them, then retracing their steps. Soon they were at the bottom of the slope. Streather and Emery had been climbing now for some hours, and they had thought they were doing well, but Jillott and Culbert seemed to catch them up very quickly. It was a measure of the very slow progress they had been making.

Emery took over the lead, followed closely by the others. Now that they were all without ice axes, Streather decided not to use the climbing rope. If one man fell, he only pulled all the others off; and while they must do all they could to stick together, they had to conserve what was left of their strength. The two falls the previous night had been terribly demoralising. Also it might not be psychologically bad for each man to know to what degree his survival depended on himself. They had to get out of the basin that day. If one of them fell back into it, the others must go on, back to Camp IV for food and drink and rest, before coming back on another rescue attempt. Otherwise it would be certain death from exhaustion and exposure for all of them.

By now, any decisions and resolutions that Streather made were not arrived at by any process of conscious thought or reasoning. They had all lost the power of reasoning and their actions were instinctive. The loss in terms of balanced judgment was less in Streather than it might be in some men. In these circumstances a formally trained mind might be a burden. The man who was accustomed to making his decisions and judgments untrammelled by lengthy thought processes and free of fixed principles or bias was at an immense advantage.

After they had climbed some 300 feet and were about a hundred feet below the platform at the beginning of the traverse, Emery suddenly saw an ice axe sticking out of the slope directly above his head. It was Culbert's, the axe Streather had been using in the second attempt to climb out last night. Emery shouted back to Streather, and Streather came through, lifted the axe out of the slope, and began cutting steps up the last hundred feet to the platform. 'You hang on here,' he told the others. 'This last bit is the worst part. When I get to the platform, I'll drop the rope to you and bring you up one by one.'

Finding Culbert's axe had been the most wonderful stroke of luck. The second of last night's falls had been in complete darkness, and in the confusion he had had no idea what had happened to the axe and had assumed had been lost in the fall. He had been feeling very apprehensive about how they would manage on the traverse. Finding the axe would make all the difference.

The last hundred feet of the slope, too, was very rotten. It was much steeper here than lower down, the surface snow tended to flake or break away, and the hard ice was not far below. Now that he had the axe he could make much better steps and there was less danger of anyone slipping off. Streather reached the platform safely, helped Emery up on the rope, and then untied and started off on the traverse, leaving Emery to drop the rope for Jillott and Culbert in turn. The traverse would be the hardest part of all and there was no time to waste: this he knew although he had lost all real sense of time. Morning, afternoon and evening were all one, indistinguishable, like colours that had run. Somewhere ahead of them lay the night; and the darkness might be complete.

It was a world of extremes: there was no light or shade. It was snowing or it was fine. It was day or it was night; it was black or it was white. They were moving forwards or backwards; there was no standing still. There was danger and there was safety. There was life and there was death, and there was nothing in between.

Emery couldn't take a belay on the platform as he had no ice axe, but he lowered the rope and took as firm a stance as he could. Then he hauled gently on the rope while Jillott and Culbert climbed up the last hundred feet.

If either of them had come off the slope he couldn't have held them, but he could have checked a slip. In fact, both men were able with the steadying aid of the rope to reach the platform safely.

They unroped and followed Streather along the traverse. Snow had blown down the slope into the steps of the traverse during the night, and Streather was having difficulty in finding the steps and cleaning them out.

The steps were slightly rising at first, where they had tried to lose height as they neared the end of the ice cliff on the way down, and suddenly Streather realised that he had come too high and that he was off the traverse altogether. Looking down the slope, he thought he could see the faint line of the old steps some twenty feet below. Cutting new steps at this higher level would take them two or three times as long, and if they were going to make any sort of progress they must regain the old line.

Streather went down the slope first, cutting and kicking the steps until he reached the original line. Back on the traverse, he didn't stop to wait for the others, but kept on cutting and cleaning out the steps. Coming down the slope was every bit as difficult for those behind, since although the steps were made, the snow was rotten and the slope was steep. Suddenly Emery, following down immediately after Streather, felt his feet slipping. He knew that to come off the traverse meant to drop over the ice cliffs again and down into the basin. He was unroped and he had no axe. He twisted his body frantically to face the slope, kept his legs rigid, and dug his crampons hard into the snow. His action served as a brake, the slide was arrested, and he went on gingerly down to the traverse. As each man came down, the steps got better, and at last they were all following Streather on the original line.

When Streather had first come down the upper slope two nights ago, he had come almost to the edge of the ice cliff before realising that he had this sheer drop directly underneath him. To the left the top of the ice cliff had risen slightly where the cliff reached its highest point above the bergschrund before falling away steadily towards the lower slope. Thus he had had to climb up slightly at the beginning of the traverse to keep above the ice cliff. Coming in this direction, the last piece of the traverse went down.

It was very awkward indeed. The steps were packed with ice, and having been cut the other way there was nothing for the toe to slide into. Each man had to make a sort of twist from the knee downwards to get a foothold. Meanwhile there was nothing they could do with their hands except use them to aid balance. The whole weight of the body was virtually being held by the crampons.

Streather was still leading, with Emery behind him, then Culbert, then Jillott. Streather and Emery started down this last piece of traverse, moving with extreme care. Once they reached the final slope and this nightmare traverse was behind them, the worst was over. But Streather hadn't gone more than twenty feet when Jillott shouted from the rear.

'Rae's in trouble.'

The difficulties under which all the climbers had been labouring had been magnified several times for Culbert throughout the day, being as he was minus a crampon and with his left foot badly frostbitten. Not once during that time had he made the smallest complaint or ever asked for help. But at this crucial point, as the traverse led obliquely down to the start of the upper slope, he stopped, unable to go further. The absolute dependence of each climber on his crampons over this last hundred feet or so of the traverse meant that Culbert, as he put his left leg forward and tried desperately hard to dig in with his right, knew for certain that he would come off.

'Do you think you could give me a belay over this bit?' he called to Streather.

'Stay where you are,' answered Streather. 'I'll give you a belay from the end of the traverse.' Emery was carrying one rope; Streather himself had the other. He tied the two ropes together to make sure of having enough, and gave one end to Culbert. Then he and Emery continued on the traverse. Eventually they reached the point directly above the ice cliff where Streather had stopped on the way down two nights ago. Above them the slope was steep, but the surface was infinitely better, there was no ice and the snow was packing beautifully. They would be able to climb up hand over hand, just as Streather and Culbert had climbed down.

Streather climbed a few feet up the slope to be sure of being on safe ground. Even now he remembered that progress of some kind was essential to their chances. 'You go on up the slope,' he told Emery. 'We'll follow as soon as we've got Rae across the traverse.'

Emery moved off up the slope and Streather turned to the business of the belay. The 200 feet of rope had been only just enough. Even with the rope, that downhill traverse would mean an agonising few minutes for Culbert, and indeed for all of them. The rope would help to steady Culbert, give him something to hang on to, but only a remarkably good belay would hold if he came off.

As soon as Streather had his axe firmly embedded he shouted to Culbert to begin. Culbert managed the first step or two, but only as a man falling downstairs will feel the first few steps pass under him. Almost immediately he came off.

He swung through space in a wide pendulum, down the slope and over the edge of the ice cliff, until he was directly below Streather. At this point his weight came on the rope. The jerk was terrific. Streather had seen and heard nothing, but he could feel himself losing his balance and slipping. Soon he was falling as in a dream, silently, a fall without an end, seemingly into nothingness. Then the illusion was shattered as a white blanket suddenly reached up and grabbed him roughly, rolling him on down the slope and finally bringing him to rest. He knew that Culbert was somewhere near him, but how he knew this was not clear.

Streather and Culbert had fallen the lower half of the avalanche fall suffered by Jillott and Emery, but the shock had been much greater because they hadn't had the great weight of snow falling with and around them that had helped to cushion Jillott and Emery. Both men were now back in the snow basin, utterly exhausted and badly concussed.

Jillott, standing behind Culbert on the traverse, had watched it all happen. Now he began on the last few steps of the fatal traverse. When at last he reached the bottom of the upper slope, he peered down over the ice cliffs towards the point where he knew Streather and Culbert must be. He was surprised to find that he was peering into darkness. Another day had gone.

He began to shout down into the basin, down into the blackness. 'We'll go on back to camp and get some food. We'll come back and help you as soon as we can.'

Streather, still dazed by the fall, heard a voice from the far end of a long tunnel, a voice yet so clear that he could feel the sibilance of it in his ear. He heard it subconsciously, and it registered subconsciously. It was like being sound asleep and yet hearing a voice in the room.

Streather clung to the words and let them revolve in his mind until consciousness returned. After the shock of the fall the darkness seemed inevitable. He realised that they were just below the bergschrund. He dragged himself up the slope, and Culbert followed. They found a point where the crevasse was filled with snow, toppled themselves over the lip and into the crevasse for shelter, and huddled together.

'Are you all right?'

'Yes. And you?'

'I'm all right.'

They had no strength to say more. They were past the stage of caring for their hands or their feet, and they sank at once into a merciful but uneasy sleep. They would wake for the morrow, but this would be their last night.

12

THE TRACKS DIVIDE

After Jillott had shouted down into the basin to Streather and Culbert, he began to follow Emery up the slope. Emery, meanwhile, was making good progress. As often seemed to happen to them during these days, he suddenly found a new lease of energy. It was partly because the snow surface on the upper slope was so much better, and partly the psychological effect of doing something constructive again. He was going well.

He was climbing up the slope in much the same way as Streather had climbed down, but the steps Streather had made had mostly disappeared and he was forced to make new ones. He pulled himself up with a crawling movement and kicked the steps out with his feet as he went. The darkness didn't trouble him. In some places the snow was too brittle and it crumbled when he tried to fashion steps, but when he reached these points he moved out to the right or left and clawed and kicked new steps where the snow was firm. His progress was slow but fairly direct and he was gaining height steadily.

He had been climbing for quite a long time and had reached a point about a hundred feet above the ice cliffs when he heard a shout from below. He waited for a few minutes, expecting to see Streather, and then to his surprise he was joined by Jillott, who told him what had happened.

The irony of this reversal of their situations – rescuers in the basin and rescued on the upper slope – was so unbearable that they couldn't discuss it. They continued silently up the sloping wall of snow that towered above them, deeply aware of the dependence of the two men in the basin on their efforts in the next few hours.

They climbed purposefully and well, concentrating only on the task in hand, until, as they neared the top of the slope, they remembered that there was one point of paramount importance – they must hit the ridge at the point where they had originally come through the cornice, otherwise they might stumble straight through the cornice in the darkness. This meant aiming for a point a little to the left of the Cardinal's hat below which they had been avalanched. It was now intensely dark and they weren't quite sure what line they were on.

'I think we ought to go slightly to the left or maintain our present line,' said Emery. Jillott disagreed – he thought they had come too far to the left and ought to veer slightly right. 'All right,' said Emery, 'we'll try your line.' He was leading, and he began to swing a little to the right. In fact Jillott proved to be wrong and they came out exactly at the point of the avalanche.

Hitting the ridge at this point had one advantage in that at least they knew which way to turn. They couldn't be more than fifty or sixty feet from the break in the cornice, but in the intense darkness they could see nothing. Emery led off along the ridge. He had taken no more than three or four paces when he went straight through the cornice.

As he fell his mind rotated like a roulette wheel, feverishly trying to alight on the answer to the question of what had been the other side of the cornice. What was he going to hit or fall into? It was infinitely worse than his fall into the crevasse that day below Camp IV, because every nerve in his body had been tensed for it then, he had been roped, and he had still had his ice axe. It almost seemed worse than the fall in the avalanche. He might be falling to his death; and even that he felt he could bear if only he knew about it.

In fact he fell no more than thirty feet, and the shock of hitting the ground so soon caught him unprepared. He landed awkwardly, and found that he couldn't get up.

He called up to Jillott. 'I'm OK, but I think my hip's gone again.' As before, it was extremely painful and he couldn't move for a minute or two, but again he happened to turn the right way and it jumped back into its socket.

'Keep going along the ridge,' he called up to Jillott. 'I'll meet you at the cut in the cornice.' Emery climbed unsteadily through the gap, Jillott made his way gingerly along the ridge, and soon both men stood at the point where, two and a half days earlier, they had gazed for the first time on the elusive secrets of Haramosh.

Somewhere here, they knew, Streather and Culbert had left their rucksacks. They began to kick about in the snow, until at length they found them. In one of the rucksacks they knew there was a water bottle. After all this time the water in it would be frozen solid. They knew this beyond doubt. And yet both men went straight for the water bottle, hoping unreasonably that somehow the water might still be liquid. One wasn't satisfied with the evidence of the other. Both men tore frantically at the water bottle just in case.

They began to search feverishly for food. In one of the rucksacks was a packet of glucose tablets. It was dark and their fingers were numb. In their haste and confusion they searched one rucksack several times but hardly disturbed the other. They were incapable of tackling the task systematically and they both searched the same rucksack. They didn't find the glucose tablets.

Jillott picked up the rucksack they had searched so vainly and shouldered it. It wasn't worth burdening themselves with both rucksacks, but they would need one to carry food and drink back to Streather and Culbert, and there might not be one at Camp IV. There was also a rope with the rucksacks, and they took this, though they decided not to rope up.

Having no ice axes, if one of them fell he would simply pull the other with him and they would both be in trouble. They felt no compunction about being unroped. Going down unroped was something they had done many times when climbing together and they were perfectly used to it.

They climbed down through the cut in the cornice, felt their way down the slope, and jumped across the crevasse. At this point Emery's dysentery troubled him again and he had to stop. Then they began to look for the route on. To begin with they knew they had to go along the lower lip of the crevasse before branching off to the left. It was very difficult indeed – they could see absolutely nothing, and they felt their way along apprehensively for several minutes. Then Emery stopped.

'I think we ought to sit down here till the moon comes up,' he suggested. 'It can't be long before it does – two hours at the most.' They'd sat through two nights now; they could easily manage another two hours. 'When the moon comes up we shall be able to see fairly well.'

'I think we ought to go on,' said Jillott. He couldn't bear to waste time here when they might be making progress towards Camp IV, and he was obsessed with the urgent need to strengthen themselves with food and drink and get back as quickly as possible to Streather and Culbert. 'I'm certain we ought not to wait. We've got to go on.'

Emery was extremely weak physically now; and he found that in this state, at this height, faced by a man who seemed absolutely certain of what they ought to do, he couldn't hold out for long. Obviously they had to keep together at all costs. He gave in, and they started off.

Jillott could move very quickly downhill, and he soon went ahead. It was characteristic of Jillott to forge ahead; and Emery, less obsessed with the extreme urgency of getting back to Camp IV, and therefore more conscious of the difficulties of the route and the importance of sticking to it, went more slowly. Jillott was moving over ground that he had seen for the first time only thirty-six hours earlier, but he was finding the way extremely skilfully. It seemed to Emery that things were going well after all.

They were on the proper route, and at this rate they would reach Camp IV in little more than an hour. And from Jillott's viewpoint there was no reason why he should worry because Emery was a bit behind. Emery knew the route far better than he did.

Soon they reached the point where the route made a wide detour to the right to avoid the patch of crevassed ground. They could see nothing, but Emery sensed that this was where they were. Here Jillott ignored the detour and went straight on, making a beeline for Camp IV. Emery shouted after him, but he had got too far behind to make himself heard. Again Emery felt that the best thing to do was to follow.

Soon after leaving the original route Emery found himself descending a very steep slope. He remembered that he had looked at this line with Culbert three days ago, and that at the bottom of this slope was a large crevasse, as one would expect at the change of levels. They had decided against it then and begun on the detour. Now he wondered how Jillott was faring and how he would negotiate the crevasse.

He could just see Jillott's tracks winding on ahead, but halfway down the slope he came to bare ice. Probably Jillott had kicked off the surface as he went down. Almost immediately Emery came off the slope and began falling, down towards the crevasse. Then came oblivion.

He couldn't remember how it had happened, but he was back at base camp now, dreaming – dreaming a nightmare in which he seemed to have fallen into a crevasse. He couldn't understand why he couldn't somehow break out of this dream. Often, in a nightmare, one was able to tear oneself out of it, like coming to the surface out of a deep dive; and he knew he ought to be able to do this now. Yet somehow he couldn't do it, he couldn't thrust the nightmare away from him; it went on and on and he was still in the crevasse. But all the time he had the comforting assurance that after all it was really only a dream, that he was back at base camp having a nightmare. It helped him to relax into oblivion.

When he awoke again it seemed to be daylight. His mind was working very slowly now and it was an effort to think at all. He began to doubt whether in fact he was really at base camp, whether in fact he had been dreaming. Part of his mind guessed that it wasn't a dream, that the safety of base camp was still remote and unattainable. He was in a crevasse, stuck where the walls had begun to converge and were narrow enough for his body to have jammed between them. The crevasse seemed to go a long way down, and below him it opened out again. It was just narrow enough for him to stick there, one leg twisted out to one side, the other hanging limply down. He was caught and somehow pinned at the pelvis, and suddenly he was conscious of pain.

Gradually he managed to prop himself up and ease his position, and by jamming himself with his crampons against one wall and with his back against the other, he was able to sidle his way along the crevasse. Suddenly the walls seemed to widen, and he half climbed and half fell through an opening. He realised that due to a depression in the slope the crevasse must be opening out on to the mountain, at some point lower than the point where he'd fallen in. He could see the surface about twenty feet above him, and he could see that by climbing on what seemed to be frozen snow debris sticking to the walls of the crevasse he could probably get out. Without an axe he couldn't test the snow to make sure it would hold him, but he trod gingerly on the patches that looked likely to hold and eventually he found his way to the surface. He crawled a little way from the crevasse, and fell asleep again.

When he awoke it seemed to be about mid-morning, possibly noon. The sun was very bright, sparkling on the snow, and the crystal glare struck painfully at his eyes. He squinted into the whiteness, and there about ten feet away were Jillott's tracks, showing up plainly in the snow. Somehow Jillott must have crossed the crevasse safely last night. He got into the tracks and followed them.

His progress now was slow and spasmodic. He would drag himself forward for twenty or thirty yards and then sink down into the snow to rest for a few minutes, and then begin again. Jillott seemed to have avoided the difficulties of the route with great skill. He came to two crevasses where Jillott had traversed along the upper lip in each case before finding a safe crossing; and the whole area was dangerously crevassed and broken. Jillott must have managed all this in the darkness last night.

The tracks came out about halfway up the last snow slope above Camp IV, the slope they had originally crossed higher up, just below the lip of the crevasse. Looking up to his right he could see the old tracks, still faintly visible; but the tracks ahead of him suddenly stopped.

The snow was deeply disturbed just in front of him, and he could see that Jillott must have slipped and come off as soon as he began across the slope. He could see the broad furrow where Jillott had slithered down; and looking down the slope he could see Jillott's tracks start again at the bottom. Evidently Jillott hadn't hurt himself much in the fall.

Emery knew that he hadn't the strength to climb up to the old track, and he didn't want to follow Jillott down to the base of the slope. The snow across the middle of the slope looked firm, and at the far end of the slope it joined the old track down to Camp IV. He began to traverse across the slope, about halfway between the old track at the top and Jillott's at the bottom. Presently he saw that Jillott's track was climbing slightly to meet the old track at the edge of the ridge above Camp IV, just below the point for which he was aiming himself.

He completed the crossing of the slope, joined the old track, and started down the ridge. This was the ridge on which they had climbed that first day above Camp IV. To his right was the deep crevasse, opening out lower down into the Stak Valley, and he kept well back from that side. To his left he could see Jillott's tracks coming up to meet him. Directly below him now he could see the snow bridge across the crevasse and then the two tents of Camp IV.

He reached the point where Jillott's track joined the track he was on. Here he expected the old track to be very much fresher, as Jillott must have followed it down to Camp IV. But the track ahead was still old and only faintly visible.

Looking down at his feet he saw that Jillott's footmarks went straight across the old track, which he must somehow have missed in the darkness. The footmarks went on for five or six feet until they reached the edge of the ridge, and there they ended. At that point the ground fell away absolutely vertically.

There wasn't even a flurry of snow to indicate that Jillott had realised that he had crossed the old track and reached the point where the ridge fell away. He must have walked straight over.

Emery stood for a moment stupefied, unable to grasp or accept the irrefutable truth that stared back at him from the footprints. He looked in vain for some sign of footmarks leading away from the edge. There was a sheer drop the other side of 300 feet into the crevasse. At the bottom one would hit ice or possibly rock. Even if the fall only knocked one unconscious, one would be shot out of the crevasse lower down and fall 6,000 feet into the Stak Valley. It wasn't a vertical drop, but there was nothing to stop or break one's fall.

When the truth finally penetrated his bemused brain, Emery absorbed it completely, with its terrible implication. Jillott was dead.

Even so, he stepped forward to a point as near the edge as he dared and shouted Jillott's name several times. He did not expect an answer, and none came.

He turned away from the edge of the ridge and began following the old track down to Camp IV, snug in the hollow below. There was a finality about Jillott's end, like a fine road that suddenly disappears in a landslide, that blunted the imagination. That Jillott was dead he knew, but the tragedy of it was too big and terrible to comprehend. In the last few days he had faced death with Jillott, calmly and without regrets or recriminations; and then all four of them had faced death together. Then he and Jillott had escaped from the basin, and their own safety had seemed assured, at least until they went back for the others. Jillott's death now was shocking and unreal. The physical fact of it registered, but his fevered mind boggled at the anguish of it. Jillott, then, was the first to go. He wondered if any one of them would get off the mountain alive.

His first thought when he reached Camp IV was to get something to drink. In the past three days he had sometimes melted snow in his mouth, but one got surprisingly little that way. From handfuls of snow one got no more than a few drops of water. The taste was extremely unpleasant, and the loss of body heat was dangerous. So that for three days at high altitude, when the very act of breathing was desiccating the whole body, he had drunk virtually nothing. But everything at Camp IV would be frozen, and to light a Primus would take a long time. He didn't have any matches, and any he could find in camp would certainly be damp. So he rummaged around in the snow outside the tents for the stores, and eventually found a tin of grapefruit juice. It would be frozen, but it would melt down into fluid in his mouth.

He crawled into the yellow tent and found a small tin opener, and tried to open the tin. Apart from a short period when he had worn a pair of socks on his hands, they had been uncovered ever since the avalanche fall, and they were now completely numb. His fingers closed around the tin opener, but he felt nothing. In order to get some sort of purchase he had to grip the tin with his free hand, using the sides of his fingers, which seemed to have retained a tiny sense of touch if not of feeling. He put his weight on the tin and began to press on the tin opener, guiding it with his wrist. As he did so, he saw in a strangely detached way that strips of skin were peeling off his fingers, revealing a sort of red jelly underneath. He hardly realised that it was happening to his own fingers. It didn't hurt at all.

He scooped out about half the frozen juice with the tin opener, and as it turned to liquid in his mouth and he drank it down he began to feel better. He decided to try to get a Primus going. He struggled out to the dump again, found a Primus, and crawled back into the tent with it.

But when he got inside he collapsed and fell asleep instantly just as he was, still in his overboots and crampons, without even crawling into a sleeping bag. He slept soundly for some hours.

When he awoke it was late afternoon, and his mind was fairly clear. He remembered that Jillott was dead. There was nothing he could do for him. He remembered that they had left Streather and Culbert in the basin. He didn't really know yet whether he would be able to go back to help them, but he still kept this in his mind as something he had to do, though in his heart he realised it was probably beyond him. He remembered how difficult it had been for Culbert with only one crampon, and he couldn't think how Culbert was going to get out of the basin. About Streather he had absolutely no doubt at all. Streather would get out. They would then go back for Culbert.

He started to work on the Primus, but his fingers were numb and torn and the matches were damp. He couldn't seem to get the stove adequately primed. Finally after over an hour he got it going. He had used two boxes of matches in the process. He melted some snow in a dixie and made himself a drink. His mouth was almost unbearably painful, swollen from eating snow and cracked and bleeding where the skin had parted through swelling and desiccation. But again he felt much better for having taken liquid. He began to melt some more snow down with the idea of making soup.

It was almost dark now. He relaxed back on to the sleeping bag. Suddenly he heard steps outside, followed by a shout. He turned to look out of the tent. He was quite certain it was Streather.

13

FIGHTING FOR LIFE

The next thing Streather was fully conscious of was that he was lying in the bergschrund with Culbert and that it was daylight. He crawled out of the crevasse and Culbert followed. Culbert was very groggy now and his left foot was almost completely useless. They moved across to the foot of the lower slope, but it was bitterly cold and blowing hard, they had been without their eiderdown jackets for two and a half days, and Streather decided that it would be folly to attempt to climb out of the basin before the sun was up. They got back into the crevasse at the point where they'd found shelter two nights before, and huddled together on the ledge, trying to sleep again.

Suddenly Streather, lingering between sleep and consciousness, thought he heard shouting. He told Culbert to stay where he was, and then climbed out of the crevasse again. He had no idea of time now, but everything seemed to have got lighter and whiter since he went back into the crevasse, and the wind had dropped. He thought perhaps he had dreamt that someone was shouting, and then looking along the far side of the crevasse to a point well beyond the lower slope he saw two dark specks which he took to be Jillott and Emery. He couldn't understand how or why they had got over there. They had evidently traversed much too far and gone right on beyond the point where the ice cliffs petered out, until they had reached a further line of ice cliffs. They seemed to be standing in a most dangerous place, right underneath these far ice cliffs, directly in the path of an almost continual avalanche. He shouted up to them, but the distance was too great and they seemed to take no notice.

He started moving across the basin towards them, keeping below the bergschrund. It meant stumbling forward through fresh, knee-deep snow, and he kept on shouting at them as he went. Then a great piece of the overhanging ice cliff broke off and obliterated them.

He shouted again in horror, and then, as the avalanching snow subsided, he saw that the two specks were still there, exactly as they had been before. It was simply two holes in the slope.

He passed his hand across his eyes despairingly in an attempt to clear his vision. He couldn't remember when he'd lost his snow goggles, but the mistiness that kept rolling across his eyes and the smarting behind his eyeballs told him that he was suffering from snow-blindness. He went back to the crevasse for Culbert. They had better start up the slope.

He tried to do some mental arithmetic, working out how long it must have taken Jillott and Emery to reach Camp IV and how long they would be in getting back. They must have reached Camp IV last night. Then they would cook some food and get some rest. They ought to be back at the point of the avalanche by about midday. He hoped to meet them somewhere on the traverse.

He had no ice axe now, so there was no point in taking the rope. They left it in the basin. Then they half pushed and half pulled each other across the bergschrund and started up the lower slope.

Evidently it had snowed in the night, because the old steps were covered in. Streather scooped out the fresh snow until he got down to the hard frozen snow underneath. The slope here was as steep as the steepest roof, and Streather made the steps as large as he could to help Culbert. As he scooped out the snow, revealing the hardened step, he saw that each cavity was stained with bright red. He remembered that he had punched these steps himself with his clenched fists. He looked at his knuckles, and saw that they were blistered and raw.

He still had a woollen glove on his left hand and a canvas overglove or mitt, but his right hand was bare. He tried to pull the sleeve of his pullover down over it, but his left hand was so stiff that the fingers slipped and the hand wouldn't crook. He lifted his wrist to his mouth and pulled the sleeve down with his teeth.

He knew it was about 300 feet to the platform at the beginning of the traverse, and he knew they were moving very slowly. They might perhaps be halfway there. He hadn't heard anything of Culbert for a minute or so, and he looked round to make sure he was all right. Culbert had gone. Looking almost vertically down he saw that Culbert was in the basin again.

He shouted down to him, 'Are you all right, Rae?'

'Yes, I'm all right. I'll try again.'

He must have slipped and come off the slope again.

He must be terribly weak, and these falls would exhaust him utterly. Yet there was nothing else they could do but keep trying. It was useless to rope up – that only meant that both of them were weakened when one of them fell. He had no axe, and he couldn't pull Culbert out on his own. He was far too weak himself to attempt it.

He saw Culbert start again at the bottom of the slope, and he went on going slowly upwards, cleaning out the steps. He had almost reached the platform and Culbert was catching up quite well, when he looked round again and saw that once more Culbert was at the bottom.

Culbert sat where he fell, looking up the slope at Streather, unable to drag himself to his feet. There was no point in his trying the slope again now. He was clearly all in.

Streather knew how desperately hard it must have been for Culbert ever since he lost the crampon. Bit by bit this tragic misfortune had sapped all his strength. He would never have given in while he could still put one foot before the other.

Streather stood precariously on the slope, motionless, looking over his shoulder at Culbert. The only hope for all of them lay in one or other of them continuing to make progress. He had recognised this ever since the avalanche. Today they had made hardly any progress at all. It must be after midday, they hadn't even reached the traverse yet, and there was still no sign of Jillott and Emery.

'What shall we do?' called Culbert.

'Hang on where you are for a bit,' shouted Streather. 'I'll go on making the steps. The others are sure to be down soon, and then we'll be able to help you.' They would have rested and fed, they would have recovered from the avalanche fall. They would bring food and drink, and perhaps a spare crampon. They would be able to help Culbert climb out.

Streather turned again to the slope. At length he reached the platform. He looked down again to where Culbert sat, already stirring himself for yet another attempt to climb out. Then he peered despairingly across the upper slope for some sign of the others.

It was no use waiting here for Culbert. He must try to make his way back to Camp IV on his own to see what was delaying Jillott and Emery.

He began along the traverse. Loose snow had blown down into the steps and they were almost completely covered in. He could just see a vague shadow where they were. He started to try to clear the steps, but he found he could not reach the nearest one without losing his balance. The canvas mitt on his left hand was frozen hard, and he took it off and used it as a scoop. This gave him another six or eight inches' reach and just enabled him to keep his balance. He scraped the loose snow out of each step, and then put his foot into it. There was no chance to try the step first – he had to put his weight fully forward, holding on as best he could with his right hand against the slope. Every step was a gamble, waiting for the loose snow in the step to pack down under his weight and to know if he had planted his foot in the right place. It was impossible to be right every time. If he missed a step he would go straight over the ice cliff again into the basin. Another fall like that would finish him. He would never get out.

What could have happened to the others? They must surely be on their way down. He began to wonder whether perhaps something had gone seriously wrong. They would be certain to come back as soon as they'd rested and fed. Besides, he'd heard Jillott shout down to him when he'd fallen off the traverse into the basin with Culbert. Or had he dreamt it? The memory was clear, but now, bemused and snow-blind, he was certain of nothing.

If they didn't get down to Culbert soon it would be too late. Neither he nor Culbert had had anything to eat or drink since leaving Camp IV to come back for the others three days ago. Since then they'd had three nights out on the mountain.

He reached the point where Culbert had fallen off the traverse. He kept on trying to scrape out the steps, but it was even more difficult here where the traverse went down. This was the stretch he had been dreading all along. Because of the downward slope he could only reach the beginning of each step with the mitt, and as he put each foot forward he was even less sure if he was stepping in the right place. There was a hundred feet of this downward traverse, and it seemed certain that somewhere in its length he would miss his footing and fall. But at last he got to the end. Then he began up the final slope.

When he reached the point where he had belayed Culbert down the traverse, he saw something sticking out of the slope. It was the ice axe he had been using then, Culbert's axe, since his own had been lost. He was beyond feeling surprise, or pleasure, or even relief. Instinctively he recovered the axe, and subconsciously he felt renewed strength. Then, moving painfully slowly, he turned again to the slope.

There was nothing in his mind to keep him going, and very little in his body. He knew that somehow he had to get to Camp IV, and that there were powerful reasons why he must succeed, but he had almost forgotten what these were. Culbert was still in the basin, Jillott and Emery were missing, and he had to get back to Camp IV to organise help for Culbert. Otherwise his mind was as numb as his fingers.

He kept on climbing up the slope, hand over hand, never looking to see how near he was to the top, never even trying to guess; like a soul climbing Jacob's ladder. His hands were not capable of cleaning out the steps now, and he jerked his elbows into them, weakly, like a tired all-in wrestler. At last he found that he had reached the start of the avalanche, and he traversed across to the point where Culbert had belayed him down. He had reached the top.

He saw the rucksack left behind by Jillott and Emery, and he stumbled towards it, fumbling inside it for the water bottle, just as the others had done. Like them he knew for certain that the water would be frozen, but as with them thirst was more powerful than reason. Yet when he saw that the water was frozen he felt a tiny glow of satisfaction which tempered the intensity of the disappointment. Reason had been right.

He found the two packets of glucose tablets, but because of his numbed fingers he couldn't open them. Before him was food and drink, yet he could get at neither. He lodged one of the glucose packets between his fists and brought his hands up towards his mouth. Then he began to chew the paper off. He couldn't grip the packet properly, and suddenly the paper tore in the wrong direction and the tablets scattered into the snow.

He knelt down and began scooping up the snow where the tablets had fallen, shaking it to sift as much snow through his hands as he could before thrusting it into his mouth. The pain of the cold snow on his cracked lips was severe, but he crunched the mixture in his mouth and gulped it down.

He found the break in the cornice, started down the slope on the other side, and then found the strength to hurl himself over the crevasse at the bottom, landing in a heap in the soft snow beyond. He dragged himself to his feet again, and began to follow the track. Soon it seemed to lead over an unfamiliar route, striking off to the left of the original track, which was still just visible. He couldn't understand why Jillott and Emery had taken a different route, but he took the line of least resistance and followed it. In any case it must lead him to them.

It was late evening now but the light was still quite good. He came to a particularly steep pitch, and suddenly the tracks stopped. He looked down the slope and saw the track again at the bottom. Evidently the others had fallen down this slope. He started to edge his way down, but almost at once he slipped and went on sliding down. As he neared the bottom he realised that he was heading straight for a narrow crevasse. This in fact was the crevasse into which Emery had fallen. He pushed hard against the slope as he shot down towards the crevasse and flung himself away from the slope at the last minute. He just cleared the crevasse and landed heavily on the far side.

Here the tracks turned right and ran along the lower lip of the crevasse. Somehow the others must have got over. Now he could see right down to the Haramosh glacier, down to the big basin between the icefall and Camp III, but in his distracted state he couldn't orientate himself. He sensed that the route was taking a dead shortcut, and he wondered how they had managed it in the darkness last night.

Suddenly ahead of him he recognised the familiar steep slope above Camp IV. Now at last he knew where he was. The tracks seemed to lead across the middle of the slope. He began to follow them, and then suddenly for no apparent reason they divided. One track went on across the middle of the slope, while the other fell away down the slope in a groove and then continued along the bottom. It looked as though one of them had come off the slope here and then made a new track lower down.

He followed the track across the middle of the slope until it joined up with the original track on the ridge above Camp IV. Then he turned and started down the ridge. Deep in the hollow below him, on the far side of the crevasse, he could see the two tents of Camp IV. It was almost dark now.

There was no sign of any movement in camp. He crossed the snow bridge over the crevasse, and as he got near camp he started shouting for Jillott and Emery, expecting them to come out and meet him. Even in his utterly exhausted state, he could feel the joy of having reached his goal.

It wasn't until he was right in the hollow of the camp that he heard a voice from one of the tents. He pulled the entrance to the tent open and there, lying on top of his sleeping bag, still in all his climbing clothes and still wearing crampons, was Emery, obviously very shaken and completely exhausted. There was no sign of Jillott.

'Where's Bernard?'

'He's gone, Tony.'

'Gone? Gone where?'

'He's gone. He's had it. He's dead.'

'What do you mean?'

'He went straight over the crest of the ridge up there and into the crevasse. I saw his footsteps leading up to the edge. He's dead.'

'Have you called?'

'Yes.' Emery collapsed back on to the air mattress, too overcome for the moment to say more. Then he asked his own question.

'Where's Rae?'

'I don't know. I'm afraid he's still in the basin. He was very weak. He kept slipping off. I doubt if he'll get out by himself. We'll have to go back for him.'

'Yes.'

As yet neither Streather nor Emery was fully conscious of the extent of the tragedy. With Jillott dead, Emery severely frostbitten, and Streather himself enfeebled, who was to go back for Culbert?

'I'm going to call Bernard,' said Streather. 'It's just possible he might still be alive.'

He stumbled back up the slope immediately above Camp IV until he reached the snow bridge. Then he began shouting down into the crevasse.

He knew there was no chance, he knew there would be no answer, but he shouted for several minutes. Then he trudged back to Camp IV.

Jillott's tragic end after reaching safety was a catastrophe too big for either of them to contemplate. Like Emery before him, Streather found that it was something he had to accept and then thrust from his mind. He felt a numb emptiness where thoughts of Jillott had been; but there wasn't the awful sense of personal responsibility that he was feeling for Culbert. Jillott's death was as though some outside force beyond their control had struck at them. It had been a life cut short in full flow; there was nothing for the mind to dwell on except the emptiness of loss.

When Emery arrived at Camp IV, he had got into the yellow tent out of force of habit. But this tent, having been dug out after successive snowfalls, had a steep and icy slope leading down to it which made it very difficult to approach and leave. Inside, the two sleeping bags fell inwards, the floor of the tent being rounded like the bottom of a boat. The tent Streather and Jillott had brought up with them was much higher and easier to enter, and the two men moved up into it.

They began to take their crampons and overboots off, and then their climbing boots and socks. Emery was unable to manage without help from Streather. Then they examined their feet. Emery's were a blueish colour from the toes to about halfway along the foot. Streather's had a slight blue line just above the toes. Streather found some dry socks, and they put these on. He helped Emery into one of the sleeping bags, and then he put his boots on and went outside to get a Primus.

For the next few hours Streather melted snow down almost continuously in an effort to satisfy their craving for liquid. He put all kinds of things into it to make it palatable – lemonade crystals, Complan, soup, Ovaltine, Complan and Ovaltine together, and so on. Sometimes they dozed for a few minutes, but then their thirst would rouse them again and Streather would melt down more snow. And all the time they lay in agony from their frostbitten hands and feet, and from the cracked and broken skin around their mouths and noses, and the burning sand and grit that seemed to lie behind their eyeballs.

They plastered their faces with cream to try to ease the soreness and when at last they felt they had drunk enough, Streather put the Primus out and crawled into the other sleeping bag. He found some sleeping pills and they each took one. It was the first time either of them had needed one throughout the expedition. They also took antibiotics to prevent their frostbitten hands and feet from becoming infected.

They knew that various people had various theories about what one should do at this stage of frostbite. The only thing one could be fairly certain of was that nothing was likely to work. Intra-arterial injections were discredited. The remedies of the old climbers, like rubbing snow on the affected parts, were quite useless. Emery had discussed the possibility of frostbite with an expert in arterial surgery before he left England. He had been told not to go in for any sort of injection, but simply to take antibiotics and keep the body warm without overheating the affected part. If the hands were affected you could leave them outside the sleeping bag, and by keeping the body warm you got a reflex opening of the arteries in the extremities. So this was what they did.

Now they tried to sleep. Exhaustion and the effects of the sleeping pills eased their pain, but their thoughts would not leave the basin where Culbert was spending his last hours. There was no pill they could take that would ease their agony of mind.

14

DISINTEGRATION

Next morning they melted more snow down and drank large quantities of liquid, but all they were able to eat was glucose. They took antibiotics, and also some vitamin pills. For a time they kept up the pretence, at least to themselves, that they were preparing to go back for Culbert; but neither really believed in it. Emery was almost helpless – he couldn't even stand up, and Streather doubted whether he would ever get him off the mountain. To attempt to go above Camp IV again with him was unthinkable. He himself was hardly able to crawl out of the tent. Everything he tried to do exhausted him and he knew there was nothing he could do for Culbert. He hadn't been able to help him yesterday and still less would he be able to help him today.

They had all survived three nights in the open above 20,000 feet, under the worst possible conditions, and this in itself had been a near miracle. Streather thought he would not have survived a fourth night himself, and Culbert had been much weaker than him. Besides, last night Culbert had been alone. He had not only been without the warmth of another body to lie against but without the immense moral sustenance of a companion. However strong one's character might be, that made a tremendous difference.

The truth that stared them in the face, but which they still refused to accept, was that Culbert had very probably died last night. Even if he were still alive now, he would be dead before they could get to him. And what of Emery? Culbert had risked his life, had lost his life, in an attempt to save Jillott and Emery. Would it not make his sacrifice pointless and empty if one at least of these two lives were not saved?

These were the thoughts that ran through Streather's mind, in an order that was only partly coherent. The decision could not be delayed. He had to make it now, before the last of his strength finally deserted him. And he knew there was only one decision to make.

To leave a man to his fate on a mountain was something that no mountaineer ever contemplated. The tradition was as old as mountaineering, and it embraced the peoples of the hills as well as the climbers themselves. The Sherpas would never leave anyone to die. They would stay with them and die with them rather than leave them. For a man like Streather, indeed for any man, it was a terrible decision to have to make. It was a decision the necessity of which would haunt him all his life. Yet fundamentally it wasn't a decision at all. There was no choice.

If they could reach Camp III, he might succeed with Hamilton's help in getting Emery off the mountain. But he was quite incapable even of the climb up to the north-east ridge, let alone of negotiating that treacherous avalanche slope and the traverse across the top of the ice cliffs and the final slope down into the basin.

Ever since the moment of the avalanche, Streather had not spared himself in his efforts to bring the whole party safely off the mountain. He had found a way down into the basin. He had led the way out. It had been his strength and skill on which all their lives had depended. He had belayed Culbert along the last piece of the traverse knowing that if Culbert slipped the rope might steady him, but that if he fell the belay would be difficult to hold. From this point on he had pinned his faith in the promised return of Jillott and Emery, only to find on reaching Camp IV that Jillott was dead and Emery exhausted and frostbitten. This situation, shocking enough in itself, had held fatal repercussions for

Culbert. Streather had reached his goal full of hope, only to be presented with the loss of Jillott and the abandonment of Culbert as a fait accompli.

There was no tragic dilemma, no question of weighing the chances of one man's life against another's. To set off up towards the ridge would be a prodigal and pointless gesture, certain to add two and possibly three lives to those already lost. He must do what he could to save Emery. He must turn his back on Culbert.

Streather knew all this instinctively. His mind was too bludgeoned by travail and tragedy to be capable of conscious reasoning. Yet he shrank from that final act of abandonment.

He would be leaving the one man among all men for whom he would willingly have given his life. His admiration and affection for Culbert had grown throughout the expedition, until now he felt about him as he had felt about Charles Houston, the American leader of the K2 expedition. He loved him as a man loves a brother.

Like any man who has been a soldier for a long time, Streather had learnt to hide his emotions. To this extent Hamilton had been right in thinking of him as a man with a façade. To some extent, too, like any regular serviceman, he had had to learn to conform, and to this extent Hamilton had been right when he had thought of him as conformist. But these could only be criticisms if there was nothing beneath the façade, if there was no independence of thought behind the ability to conform. Emery, quick to find the best in people, had soon penetrated the façade. Culbert, with the directness of his race, had been unaware of it and had made common ground with Streather at once. These two men had talked little, but they had understood each other perfectly.

Culbert, in fact, was one of those rare people capable of making common ground with almost anyone. Each one of the climbers, in his own way, had felt a special affection for him. To each of them he had been the perfect companion. Hamilton had recognised in him an ally from the New World. Emery, like Streather, had loved him like a brother. He had given Jillott friendship when Jillott had needed a friend. And there had been this unspoken but perfect understanding with Streather. It fell to few people to be so universally loved.

Streather and Emery were still thinking of Culbert's last hours, alone in the basin. They would be able to think of little else for a long time. But for the present they were still hoping against hope that somehow Culbert might have survived. It seemed impossible to believe that he wouldn't come in just as he always did. Streather laid out a sleeping bag, a Primus and some food, and wrote him a note. It was a gesture they had to make for their peace of mind.

Now Streather began to prepare for the journey down to Camp III. He helped Emery on with his windproof clothing, but he was unable to get him in to his boots because of his swollen feet. Streather's own boots, a full size larger, were a pair of softer texture which had been specially made for the expedition to Kangchenjunga, and he gave these to Emery. Then he helped him on with his crampons. His own hands were still badly torn and benumbed and all this took a long time.

They had no means of knowing whether Hamilton had stayed at Camp III, or whether he had given them up for dead and gone down. They were several days overdue. If Hamilton had gone down, there might be no tent left at Camp III, so they would have to take one of the tents from Camp IV. It would add greatly to their difficulties, but they couldn't risk another night in the open. Streather dismantled the second tent and packed it up. Then he packed Emery's rucksack with his sleeping bag and lilo, and put in his camera and some used film. He packed his own rucksack similarly and attached a short rope to the tent so that he could drag it along with him.

Meanwhile Emery started to make an attempt to stand up by himself and to walk. He knew that if they were to get safely off the mountain he would somehow have to stay on his feet. But he found, as he had feared, that he couldn't stand unaided. The one ice axe would be far more use to them in Streather's hands, and in any case he couldn't have held it properly himself or got much support from it. He found two ski sticks which had been brought up earlier to Camp IV, and by putting his wrists in the leather thongs of these sticks and leaning his weight on them he was able to stand up and achieve some sort of balance. But when he tried to walk he fell over.

For the next few minutes, while Streather was striking camp, he tried to evolve some method of progress with the aid of the sticks. Again and again he fell into the snow; and each time he fell it seemed to become more difficult when he tried again. He was unable to grip the sticks with his hands, he could feel nothing in his feet, and his wrists slipped easily out of the thongs. When he stumbled he was unable to use his arms to recover balance, and when he fell he couldn't use his hands to break the fall. But at last, getting used to the fact that he could feel nothing in the forward part of his feet, digging in with his heels, and balancing somehow on the rest of the boot, he began to get along. Then they started down.

The tracks were still showing faintly across the narrow neck of snow where Emery had fallen into the crevasse. Streather went across first, without a belay; he left the tent and rucksack on the far side, and then came back to belay Emery across. They reached the top of the ice cliff, and then began down the steep slope leading to the Haramosh glacier. Now for the first time they could look down towards Camp III. They thought they could just see the top of a tent, but they weren't sure.

Emery led down, with Streather holding him on the rope from behind. Very slowly, half sitting and half sliding, he edged his way down. At first the snow was fairly soft, but soon they reached a point at the steepest part of the slope where the snow practically disappeared and they were on almost bare ice. Emery could make no sort of step for himself in the ice without an axe, so Streather cut a small stance for himself and then lowered Emery down for thirty feet or so. Emery then kicked as best he could until he had something to stand on, feeling nothing, and when

Streather was satisfied that Emery was secure on the slope he cut steps down to join him. Then he lowered Emery again on the rope.

Very quickly he began to find the dragging weight of the tent an intolerable burden. The danger was that he might lose his balance and pull Emery off as well. The slope here was very steep, and if they came off there was a very good chance that they would fall into a large crevassed area to their left or straight off the mountain and down into the Stak Valley to their right.

Streather decided to roll the tent down the slope in the hope that it would run straight and finish up on the glacier. He let it go, guiding it as best he could. It ran straight for two-thirds of the way, but then it struck a projection in the slope and veered sharply to the left, disappearing almost at once into a crevasse.

It was a warning of what might happen to them if they came off the slope. And it left them without hope of shelter if they failed to reach Camp III or if the tents were gone. One thing was certain. They would never survive another night in the open.

15

ALONE AT CAMP III

It was 14 September when Hamilton returned alone from Camp IV to Camp III, watched safely down the slope by Streather and Jillott. The steps had been remade that day and he climbed down easily. He was not at all resentful at being left to hold the fort at Camp III – in fact he was quite looking forward to a day or two's solitude. It was natural that the leader and deputy leader should want to take part in the climb above Camp IV, and Culbert and Emery were there already and could hardly be brought down now. In any case they knew the conditions and had earned their chance. It had never been intended that he should go to the higher camps and he was quite content with the climbing experience he had gained.

14 September was a Saturday. The others would be climbing above Camp IV all day Sunday and possibly on Monday too, but they would be back at Camp III on Monday evening, or at the latest some time on Tuesday. Then they would have to hurry if they were to meet their return bookings.

When there was no sign of the others on Tuesday, Hamilton's imagination, always fertile, began to explore the possible reasons for the delay. After a great deal of thought he decided that the issue was pretty clear-cut. At best, they might have found a route to the summit and decided to make the attempt, abandoning the existing plan for the return journey.

At worst, all four of them could have been wiped out. Between these two extremes there were endless possibilities.

Hamilton felt that the first extreme was the more likely. If there had been the chance of a route, Jillott would have wanted to take it; and Streather might be reluctant to overrule him, as he had been reluctant before. It was such a strong climbing party in skill and experience that he could not believe that an accident could have happened which made it impossible for at least one of the climbers to return.

Hamilton knew his own faults, and he knew that his imagination was apt to run away with him: in situations like this he always had to apply a governor to it. He mustn't look for spectacular reasons for the delay. Very probably there was a simple and undramatic explanation which tomorrow he would learn.

When no one appeared on Wednesday, he began to feel a conviction that something had gone wrong. It could still be nothing more than that they had gone for the summit and found the route harder than they anticipated; but he was a natural pessimist, and the conviction of tragedy grew. He knew now that he must make some sort of plan; but what in fact was the best thing to do?

To climb alone down from Camp IV in newly made steps was one thing: to climb up alone after four days had elapsed was another. Nevertheless, if no one showed up today he would have to make a quick trip up there on Thursday morning to see if there was any sign of them. If he found nothing, he would descend immediately, trying to reach base camp in one or at the most two days, climbing by night as well as day if possible. Then he would try to mount a rescue party.

But when Thursday morning came he found himself in an agony of indecision. The last few days of inactivity had affected him with lassitude, so that it became more and more difficult for him to take positive action. Suppose, after he went down from Camp III, an injured climber came in needing help? And what would be the use of a rescue party of Hunzas, who would have to carry their food and bedding up the mountain again, having almost certainly gone down by now, and who in any case had no high-altitude clothing? They might even have left base camp. It would be a week before he could get anyone above Camp IV, and what would be the good of that?

He must get a grip on his imagination, and on his tendency to pessimism. He had been left here to keep Camp III open. There was still a chance that the delay could be readily explained. Within another twenty-four hours or so he would have to go up to Camp IV to see what he could establish, but in the meantime he would spend one more day at Camp III.

The hours passed slowly. Most of the time he spent standing outside the tent, scanning the peaks of Haramosh II. Each day since Sunday he had prepared food and drink in case the others came down. Now, towards the middle of the afternoon, he again began to prepare a meal. He got the Primuses going, started the meal cooking, and then, because of the confined headroom in the tent, lay on his sleeping bag. It was warm in the tent, the Primuses purred soporifically, and soon he dozed off.

He awakened with a start to the feel of boiling water on his hand spilling from one of the Primuses, and with a dreamlike conviction that he had heard his name called. He bandaged his hand quickly, and then heard his name called again.

'Scott … Scott … ' There was no doubt about it, there was someone very near calling him, only just outside the tent. He began to pull his boots on quickly; and looking out he saw Streather, already in camp, his face contorted with pain and exhaustion, holding on to the other tent for support. Far up the route towards the col he saw a grotesque ape-like figure, hunched up and flopping his hands in front of him, which he recognised with difficulty as Emery. There was no sign of anyone else.

Hamilton called tremulously across to Streather. 'Are we safe?'

Streather began to shake his head. 'No, no, no.' It was a groan from deep within him rather than articulate speech. Hamilton stared at Streather, not daring to ask more, not needing to ask more. It was all too tragically plain.

Perhaps it was the way Hamilton had phrased the question, showing that in spite of his lone vigil at Camp III the feeling of being one of a team was still strong in him; perhaps it was the burden of the news he had survived to tell; perhaps at last he was at the end of his tether. But now Streather sank down into the snow in a state of collapse and sobbed out the names of Bernard Jillott and Rae Culbert.

'Bernard ... is dead. Poor Rae ... he kept falling off ... falling off.' His voice was choked in sobs. 'What could I do? I meant to go back for him, but there was no one to help. My strength was gone. What could I do?' His voice trailed off in a paroxysm of anguish and remorse.

Hamilton still stood agape, comprehending but unable to recover from the shock. Here before him he was seeing at last the whole man, the man from whom during the past weeks they had all drawn their strength, the man who had so nearly converted catastrophe into rescue, the man who but for the mischance of a lost crampon would have brought the whole party off safely. Here at his feet, prostrate with exhaustion and grief, was the man who had fought on and kept his courage when perhaps no other man living would have survived; the man whose dislike of emotional displays did not mean that he felt no emotion himself, whose tears for his dead comrades now fell into the snow.

16
LAST NIGHTS ON THE MOUNTAIN

Still overcome with horror and shock, Hamilton set off up the track towards Emery, who was limping with the aid of the ski sticks across the last hundred yards into Camp III. His orange high-altitude suit was soiled and crumpled, his gait was crippled, his face twisted and grotesque. His hands were so swollen and torn that he had been unable to hitch his trousers up and they were sagging and slipping, revealing a gap at the waist. 'Please pull my pants up,' he said gruffly, not looking at Hamilton, keeping his eyes fixed on Camp III. Hamilton lifted the trousers at the waist and tried to support Emery under the shoulder, but Emery brushed him aside. The old obduracy was still there. He meant to reach Camp III on his own.

When they joined Streather, Hamilton prepared to serve a meal, but Streather stopped him. 'We only want liquids, Scott,' he said. 'We can't eat.' Thick black scabs had formed on their cracked lips and any movement of the mouth caused them acute pain. They crawled into the other tent and Hamilton unpacked their rucksacks and inflated their air mattresses, and took off their crampons and boots. Throughout the evening he brought them more and more liquid and they drank it greedily but with great difficulty, holding the beakers in their cupped hands and trying not to hurt their lips. When the time came for sleep, nightmares disturbed them and they were still haunted by the picture of Culbert alone in the basin. Streather dreamt again and again that he was still crossing the traverse; Emery was back in the crevasse, fighting to remember where he was. Throughout the night Hamilton was kept awake by the half-delirious shouts that came from their tent.

Next morning there was again the protracted and tedious business of trying to pack and go down. They had many difficulties and hazards ahead of them and it was by no means certain that they would find their way through the icefall and reach Camp II in one day; so Streather decided to take a tent and a Primus just in case they had to bivouac between camps. Hamilton made some porridge, Streather helped Emery on with his boots, Hamilton strapped Emery's crampons on, and between them Hamilton and Streather took down one of the tents and packed it, and repacked the rucksacks with the air mattresses and sleeping bags. It was midday when they set out down the long snow plod into the icefall.

There was still a faint shadow where the old track had been, but it was almost completely obliterated by fresh snow. Behind them Haramosh was shrouded in mist, shutting them off from their experiences and yet somehow concentrating them in the memory. Soon the mist began to appear ahead of them and the sky clouded over. The spell of fine weather was at an end.

The snow was still very deep and the going was extremely hard and slow. Emery was able to move only a few yards at a time, every step being an achievement in itself and giving no promise of another step to follow. Eventually, in spite of the bad visibility, they reached the top of the icefall, and soon they saw the flag that Streather and Jillott had fixed at the point where the ladder crossed the big crevasse. The crevasse had opened up a lot and the ladder was only just lodged on the lower lip. Streather climbed down to try to adjust it, belayed from above by Hamilton. Eventually he crawled gingerly across on his hands and knees, and once on the far side he was able to secure it for the others. Hamilton now ferried across the rucksacks and the tent, making three crossings in all. Last of all came Emery. He had done his best to give Hamilton some sort of belay, but while he was waiting he had almost collapsed again with exhaustion and cold. Streather called up to him encouragingly. 'Come on, John, this is our last big hurdle.' This was how they braced themselves for almost every difficulty they came to.

It was late afternoon now and it seemed doubtful if they would reach Camp II. It was a good thing they had brought the tent.

The icefall, malleable as ever, had changed considerably since last they were through, but the marker flags were still standing and they pointed the way. Even so it was heavy going, and in places the crevasses had opened up and they had to move with great care. The mist enveloped them and it began to get dark. Streather was not keen on pitching the tent until they were safely through the icefall, and he led the way slowly through the maze of cliffs and crevasses. Eventually he reached the top of the steep snow slope leading down into the basin. He edged his way slowly down, feeling more insecure at each step. Then he slipped, and Hamilton, belaying him from above, was unable to hold him. All three of them slid down through the deep snow and landed in a heap in the basin a hundred feet below.

Emery fell awkwardly into a patch of loose snow. His head was buried and he felt himself suffocating, but his legs, caught up with the ski sticks, were so placed that any movement gave him excruciating pain. Streather managed to extricate him eventually. He and Hamilton had lost their ice axes in the fall. This would make the last stage of their journey off the mountain, particularly the steep slope below Camp II, more precarious even than they had feared.

They pitched the tent where they fell. Ordinarily they would have been only about fifteen minutes from Camp II, but it was dark now and their strength was gone.

They lit a Primus and made something to drink, and before they got into their sleeping bags Streather gave Emery a penicillin injection, and Hamilton did the same for Streather. At first, to give the others more room, Hamilton lay in the middle; but Streather and Emery both felt a sense of physical loss. They had suffered and struggled together and depended on each other for so long that they could not bear to be separated. The burden they shared was too great for one. Eventually Emery moved into the middle, and they slept, disturbed by bad dreams.

Next morning the cloud was low in the basin and visibility was almost nil. Slowly they began to get themselves ready for the day. The mist lifted for a moment after an hour or so, long enough for them to get a glimpse of Camp II, and Streather sent Hamilton across at once. 'Go straight to Camp II,' he said. 'Then if the mist comes down again the track will be made and we'll have something to follow. You can come back here and help us when you've made the track.'

While Hamilton was away, Streather continued to get Emery dressed and to fix his crampons. Soon Hamilton returned for them, and they made their way safely to Camp II. Here there was a comfortable tent and plenty of food left behind by the Hunzas, specially prepared before they went down. The route down to the valley would be dangerous without ice axes, and they would need a full day to do it, since Camp I had been struck and there was no intermediate camp now. Streather decided to spend the rest of the day in Camp II, eating and drinking as much as they could and having a good rest before facing the final hazards of the climb down to base camp.

He had no illusions about the next day. It would be difficult. But surely at some time they would be seen by the Hunzas, and then they could rest until help reached them. His mind moved on ahead. They would have missed their air bookings, and it was essential to their chances of recovery to get back to England quickly. Fortunately he had friends all the way back to Karachi, friends who would organise things for them and smooth their passage across Pakistan. They might well be back in England within a week.

There was very little hope for Emery's hands and feet. The fingers and toes would certainly never recover. Ahead, for Emery, lay many months of suffering and a lifetime of disability. Streather was uncertain about himself, but thought he might get away without any very serious loss. His feet were hurting badly, but the pain was probably aggravated by wearing Emery's smaller boots. The important thing was to get back to expert treatment as soon as possible.

What would become of Emery, what would happen to his career? He would never be able to pursue the normal profession of doctor, medical practitioner, surgeon. He didn't know how much this meant to Emery, but he did know that Emery, alone among all of them, was the possessor of a first-class mind. It was in the mind that the struggle would be; and few men were better equipped for it.

There would be telegrams to send, telegrams to Jillott's people in Yorkshire, to Culbert's people in New Zealand. There was nothing he could say to soften the blow, nothing he could say to tell them what he felt. Once they had shaken down, they had all got on so splendidly, and then on the last day, catastrophe, with tragedy upon tragedy to come.

First they had lost Jillott. This had been something entirely outside their control; Jillott had died after being saved, fate itself had struck at them here. He still felt the same sense of numbness over the loss of Jillott. It was like trying to understand the ways of God. But one day soon the numbness would go, and they would remember the essential Jillott, volatile and impulsive, determined and fearless, with a tremendous faith in his own ability. More than any of them, his life had been dedicated to the hills. For the rest of them, there were other things in life. For Jillott the mountains had been everything.

Was it not the desire to see over the next hill that was responsible for all mankind's progress? Was it not the urge to widen his experience that inspired and animated man's spirit? Was not mankind in eternal debt, physically and spiritually, to the Jillotts of this world?

If man's destiny was to strive to add to the sum of his experience, then Jillott's life had been creative, and his death was no senseless loss.

They would remember, too, that Jillott had lost his life in hurrying in the darkness to save others. If motives counted for anything, then Jillott had died a hero's death no less than Culbert.

Jillott was to have written a book about the expedition when he got back. His writings, published and unpublished, showed him to be a gifted writer with a keen eye for incident and colour, free from self-deception, and with a deep sense of mountain atmosphere and the companionship of climbing. His ambition to be a climber–writer would surely have been fulfilled.

For Culbert, too, there was a numbness now – the numbness caused by trying to forget how he must have spent his last hours. But there was another picture in the back of their minds, a picture they had seen when climbing on that last day from Camp IV to the north-east ridge. When they were crossing the big snow bridge over the long crevasse, Culbert had stopped to take some camera shots looking back towards K2. This had been their last clear picture of him. In everything that happened afterwards, though the incidents and their own part in them were clear, they had been too absorbed in what they were doing to get a clear picture of anyone else. On that day, Emery had produced a camera and tried to take a photograph of Culbert. Culbert was always slightly self-conscious when anyone tried to take a picture of him, and this time as usual he scowled at the camera. Emery shouted, 'Grin, you bastard, grin,' at the top of his voice, and the black beard broke, there was a flash of white teeth, and there was the grin that was entirely Rae Culbert. Slowly that grin would come into focus, and that was what they would remember.

With Culbert it was easier to find solace. He had gone into the basin to rescue his friends and had died in the attempt. But they wouldn't want to make a particular hero of him. Being what he was, there was no other way in which he could have acted. He was just Rae Culbert, he was everything that was admirable and lovable, and there would never be anyone like him.

They would discuss over and over again what other courses of action they might have taken, both before and after the avalanche. Should all four of them have climbed together on that last day? If they hadn't, then two of them might have been avalanched and might never have been found. Could they perhaps have passed a crampon back to Culbert on that last part of the traverse? Their hands had been completely benumbed then, fixing and unfixing a crampon would have taken a long time, and anyway would have been physically impossible on that steep slope. Could Emery have restrained Jillott from pressing on ahead into the darkness? It was almost certain that Jillott's sense of urgency was right, that only a quick return to the basin with food and drink could have saved Culbert. Should Emery perhaps have roped up with Jillott? There was one good reason for doing so – it would have kept them together. But there had been valid reasons against, outweighing this one. Should Streather have stayed in the basin with Culbert? Had he done so, he could have done nothing for Culbert, he would have been too weak in another twenty-four hours to climb out himself, Emery would have died at or near Camp IV, and even Hamilton would almost certainly have failed to get off the mountain. They would inevitably conclude that to climb at all, as to live at all, meant exposing oneself to danger. There had been an accident, and two of their comrades had forfeited their lives.

It was a pathetic little party that struggled across the col next day and down the snow slope leading towards the old site of Camp I. Hamilton was leading now. Up to this point he had been too overcome by the tragedy to take the initiative. To have been through these things, to have suffered with their comrades, somehow made it more bearable for Streather and Emery. But for Hamilton, learning the truth at second hand, after a long period of anxiety and inactivity, the effect had been to render him physically and mentally incapable of taking over the leadership.

The blow had inflicted on him a sort of mental concussion. But now he had recovered, and he took over the lead.

They had been late in leaving Camp II. Streather had been determined that they should have something to use in place of ice axes on the steep slope, and they had dug out two aluminium stakes which were keeping up the tent. They had had to use plates as shovels, and it had taken a long time to free the stakes. The morning was well advanced when they started.

Hamilton had spent a lot of time in the early days of the expedition working on this part of the route, and he knew it well. But when the slope steepened they had to belay each other with the aluminium stakes all the way, and this made progress terribly slow. When they had been fit and fresh they had managed this slope easily; now it seemed almost impossibly steep. If they made a mistake they had no powers of recovery, and they inched their way down.

So much snow had fallen in the past few weeks that the old route was completely obliterated, and many of the rocks that had protruded before were now snow-covered, so that it was difficult to recognise where they were. Streather and Emery were unable to use their hands, so rock climbing was out of the question. They tried to keep to the snow gullies, but in places the snow surface was treacherous, and it seemed that they were still a long way from safety.

Four thousand feet below them, in the valley, they could see the Mani glacier and the shepherds' huts at Kutwal Sar. Everything looked strange and still, and the valley seemed deserted. So far from getting help from the Hunzas, it suddenly struck Streather that Sahib Shah and the porters might have given them up for dead, and that base camp might have been evacuated.

The whole valley seemed to have undergone a fundamental change. Streather looked again, and saw that the green slopes had turned brown, that the whole colourful valley was now arid and lifeless. He wondered whether the shepherds might have left their summer grazing grounds and moved on down the valley. It was getting late in the year, and at this altitude winter could not be far away. It looked as though, when they reached base camp, they might find themselves forced to trudge all the way down to Iskere. He doubted if they had the strength to do it.

Darkness was upon them and they were still nowhere near the rock island on which they had sited Camp I, let alone base camp. Streather and Hamilton got their torches out to look for the route, but it was hopeless. It seemed that they would never find a place to rest. At last they came to a small piece of flat rock about six feet square where Streather thought it might be possible to bivouac for the night. They cleared away the loose rocks and built up the sides of the platform until there was just room to put down two air mattresses. Then they put the three sleeping bags on top, crawled in, and settled down under the open sky for their last night on the mountain.

It was relatively warm at this height and it was nothing after the hardships they had been through. When they awoke next morning it was snowing steadily and they were lying under a white blanket of snow, but they were warm in their sleeping bags, and they waited until the sky cleared and the sun appeared over the Haramosh La before starting down on the last stage of the climb to safety.

As they prepared to go, the climbing rope caught Emery's rucksack and dislodged it from the little platform. It began to fall quickly down the slope, bouncing from rock to rock, charging down at full tilt, until eventually it crashed down on to the glacier 2,000 feet below. In the lost rucksack had been all the film Emery had taken, daily throughout the expedition, to make a study of the blueing of the lips at altitude. But in one way the loss of the rucksack was a blessing, as Emery was relieved of its weight. Movement was agony for Streather and Emery, and they both moved painfully slowly. All the time they looked for some sign of life in the valley, but they saw none, not even an animal. It seemed that their struggle would start again from base camp.

By midday they seemed to have made very little progress; and then suddenly they thought they saw movement on the scree slopes 1,000 feet below. They stopped in their tracks and waited. Soon, as the figures moved on to a surface of snow, their silhouettes became clear. They couldn't yet recognise them individually, but they knew it must be the Hunza porters, Dhilap Shah, Rustam, Shakoor Beg, Nadir, Nadil and Johar, leaning into the slope and kicking steps with fast but measured rhythm, hurrying up to meet them.

Once the compulsion to move was gone, the ability to move was gone. Only now did Streather and Emery realise how near they were to the end. They could go no further. They sank down into the snow, watching the Hunza porters, strong and fresh and full of the promise of help and succour, climbing purposefully up towards them, rapidly closing the gap.

AFTERWORD

Haramosh was climbed in 1958 by an Austrian expedition. The long ridge from the scene of the avalanche to the summit took them eight days to overcome.

Tony Streather returned to the Gloucestershire Regiment, and rose to the rank of lieutenant colonel before retiring in 1977. His military service included postings to Cyprus, Berlin and Northern Ireland, and a secondment with the 6th Gurkhas in Hong Kong. In 1976 he led the successful Army Mountaineering Association expedition to Everest. He received an MBE in 1965 and an OBE in 1977, and was president of the Alpine Club from 1990 to 1992. He died in 2018 at the age of ninety-two.

John Emery withstood a painful convalescence, qualified as a doctor and eventually returned to serious mountaineering in the early 1960s despite the disability of severely maimed hands. He wrote about his continued passion for climbing in 'The Runcible Cat', a much-praised paper originally read to the Alpine Club in March 1961 and reproduced in the following pages as the Appendix. He was killed while descending the Weisshorn in 1963.

APPENDIX

'THE RUNCIBLE CAT'
BY JOHN EMERY

(A paper read to the Alpine Club on 7 March 1961.)

With apologies to Edward Lear I want to begin by quoting from 'The Pobble who has no toes':

'The Pobble swam fast and well
And when boats or ships came near him
He tinkledy-binkledy-winkled a bell
So that all the world could hear him.
And all the Sailors and Admirals cried,
When they saw him nearing the further side,—
"He has gone to fish, for his Aunt Jobiska's
Runcible Cat with crimson whiskers!"

But before he touched the shore,
The shore of the Bristol Channel,
A sea-green Porpoise carried away
His wrapper of scarlet flannel.
And when he came to observe his feet,
Formerly garnished with toes so neat,
His face at once became forlorn
On perceiving that all his toes were gone!'

Most of you will know the hills north of Ullapool. The land there has a curiously primeval quality of age and youth, a timeless mood of 'as it was in the beginning': a flat wilderness of heather and gorse, merging almost with the sea, sweeps in from the coast to meet those extraordinary hills, thrusting up from the flat world like sleeping monsters. On a day last spring three of us were climbing on one of these hills, Stack Polly. The narrow western end of the mountain stands like the tower of a fortress, smooth and abrupt, looking out to the sea, but as we climbed it that day, edging up over the great blocks of sandstone which form its walls, I felt no response to the rush and leap of the rock. Instead I was at variance with the mountain, the old harmony had gone and I found only a dull and leaden unhappiness, a sort of puzzled frustration which had hung on me for several days. At about two-thirds height of the buttress, rounding a flake we came to a small incut corner, like a window embrasure on the face of the tower; at the back of the corner was a crack and this was evidently the only way up. The lower part of the crack was smooth and holdless so I moved round on to the ledge which made a window-sill at the foot of the corner. I wedged my back into the corner and pressed my hands against its opening walls, then Michael Williams, who was leading, stepped up on to my shoulder. As he stood there a moment I stiffened to meet the surge and pressure of the rock about me, against my back, my shoulders, my hands and my feet. For a few moments I could put my strength against the mountain, and as I did so I could feel the wind eddying up the face below me, smell the dry rock beside me, and look across the world to the sea and the islands. Mike moved up but the moment did not pass, for I had regained something from it which stayed with me during that day and has remained with me since. It was an end and a beginning, although I did not realise it then, a change in my attitude to mountains, and I have described it because this is an entirely personal enquiry. So elusive a thing as a mountaineering philosophy is almost impossible to define for oneself; to attempt to do so for others would be presumptuous. What follows is simply one man's wanderings amongst all men's hills.

For many years before I began to climb, I had felt strongly attracted to mountains in a way which I could not explain, for I had no yardstick of experience with which to define it. I tried walking in the hills but found it disappointing; always there was a hint in the tilting perspective, a catch of anticipation which would not reveal itself. Eventually, however, I came to climb and the hills fulfilled their promise. I had discovered an extension of experience that moved and excited me beyond description; it was as exhilarating as a moment many years before, in a dusty classroom, when I first read Shaw's *Major Barbara*, and suddenly realised that it was possible to think for oneself!

After that the world opened up like an oyster. There was always the next route to climb and a friend to climb it with; Wales gave way to the Lakes, Zermatt was round the corner and then Chamonix blinded me with its brilliance. It was an uncomplicated progress towards an ever widening horizon; always an adventure, a physical and mental adventure. Physically there was the climb, the struggle, the movement on the mountain with all that this entailed of rhythm and technique and muscular well-being; complementary to this was the mental attitude necessary for the climb itself, and beyond it were great beauty, friendship, and the mental results of the struggle. These three last were the important reasons for climbing, of that I was sure, but I have said that they were beyond the physical act of climbing and could only be reached through it. Because of this, the quality of the climb was important. Most of us would say that we get more kick out of a VS route than doing the Milestone Ordinary. I climbed to the limits of my ability because in so doing I could extend the limits of my experience. I could find out more about myself and about my friends when the situation was sharpened by difficulty, while the beauty revealed was always intimately related to the total quality of the experience, for I don't believe in art *dégagé* whether in looking at paintings or mountains; the concept of a sort of disembodied aesthetic makes me want to laugh.

My perception was conditioned by physical circumstance and the resulting mental awareness, and this awareness went beyond the mountain, with me when I stepped back through the looking glass again, to bring pleasure to the contrast of everyday things and a renewed sense of proportion to the values of everyday life. All this depended to a greater extent than I realised on the physical act of climbing and the uncomplicated enjoyment of the climb itself. Technique was never more than a means to an end. A passion for thirty-foot outcrops or stone railway bridges seemed dismally small-minded, but technique was a necessary touch-stone: it led to the special freedom and through that to the particular vision which each route unlocked. Perhaps the strongest of these attitudes of mind, and the one which I looked for most often, was the overwhelming access of humility which came at the completion of a hard climb. Eckhart says that 'if the soul knows God in His creatures, that is only evening light'; nevertheless it was light, and strong enough to search for again and again. Mountains, then, were an obvious challenge, not to any element of conquest, for the idea of conquering mountains was ludicrous, nor to the Spirit of Man which could be left to Sir Francis Younghusband or anyone else who cared, but to a sort of restless curiosity about the total of mountain experience. The curiosity, however, was unrestrained; what was dangerous about it was the naïvety of the underlying assumption that the nature of mountain experience would only be revealed through the extremes of action on the mountain.

This headlong rush of eager enquiry was halted three years ago, when circumstance, in the form of frostbitten fingers and toes, imposed a period of comparative inactivity upon me and administered what should have been an effective astringent to my thinking on the subject of mountains. The lesson, however, was learned slowly; others would have made the obvious change of attitude more quickly, or would have avoided the false position in the first place. I had no hesitation in wanting to climb again; I had always considered that anyone who stops climbing after a mountain accident, unless compelled to do so by physical incapacity, has no business to be climbing in the first place, because he has either failed initially to consider the full implications of mountaineering, or else has wilfully blinded himself to them. That I would be able to climb in some fashion I had no doubt either, because I had the splendid example of Robin Hodgkin in front of me. I would only be able to climb easy rock now, and snow and ice were unknown quantities depending on how much grip I would have for an axe or ice hammer, but the important thing was that I would be able to climb somehow. So this future limitation in ability was not difficult to come to terms with; I could accept it quite early on. Of course I realised that it would be more painful when I actually returned to the hills and saw what I had once climbed, but the initial step of acceptance had been made. What I failed entirely to do, however, was to realise the effect that this would have upon my attitude to mountains, upon the ultimate enjoyment I drew from them. I did not see that my altered climbing ability would demand a fundamental change in my attitude if I was to continue to find happiness in the hills. So far from making this next, most important, step was I, however, that I simply thought of mountains with a sort of non-specific longing, an unreasoning belief that all would be well when I was back amongst them; to make sure that all would be well when I was back amongst them demanded a degree of insight and resilient thinking which I made no effort to find. I was taking refuge in an idealised fiction; climbing and mountains, when I thought of them, began to take on something of the unreality of climbing dreams, becoming a sort of poetic progression over limitless hills; how I arrived in these situations was just left conveniently unsolved. It was, in fact, a misty emotional abstraction, a sort of model which I had constructed. It had its uses but the danger was obvious, as Professor Edgar Wind pointed out in a recent Reith Lecture when, dealing with the treatment of art as if it were pure, he said, 'There is no harm in moving among such abstractions as long as the model is not confused with the thing', and he went on to quote from *The Circus Animals' Desertion*:

'Players and painted stage took all my love
And not those things that they were emblems of.'

The first hill that I returned to was small, grassy and had a large pylon on top; about as undramatic as it could possibly be. Nevertheless it was enough for me that day because I put on a pair of boots and walked uphill for the first time. That was simple but clear pleasure, just the movement upwards. Later, I returned to Wales. The first touch of November mist and the smell of my anorak as I pulled it on, eloquent of bog and slime and other men's socks, was enough to drive away the hospital fog of abstract mountains. We walked up Cwm Idwal; I was with Mike Mee again. Last time it had been the long slanting elegance of the West Buttress of Cloggy, today it would be the Ordinary Route on the Slabs, wet and tightly shrouded in mist. My mind was an odd jumble of hope and apprehension. In that familiar setting with the rope snaking up behind Mike, I really couldn't get rid of the feeling that anyone ought to be able to run up the Ordinary with both hands tied behind his back; indeed it was all faintly comic but it would be a good problem. In fact, it took just five seconds on the rock to hammer out the pattern of things to come. The first hundred feet was a grotesque mockery of groping bewilderment; the looking glass smashed to splintered pieces and the fragments ran down the streaming rock.

A hundred feet up there was a belay and a pause, time to look around and time to throw overboard the tattered shreds of the past and start right at the beginning again. There was a new discipline to be learned, an old one to be forgotten. Curbing the old, confident automatic movements was the difficulty. Now it was a fist, the palm or side of the hand, push not pull; I feel like a rather backward seal attempting to climb on to the ball at the circus. Mike waited patiently in the rain above while I pottered, swore, clutched and shoved. It was slow but it was working, and as I moved up I began to find a secret pleasure in carefully and methodically breaking all the classic rules of rock climbing in one afternoon.

That was a day in isolation, but it was a beginning, and the first hundred feet was a long way behind. Inevitably, however, it meant that when I returned again my first concern would be with technique; the bigger problem would be obscured for a time.

There followed a long interval of impatient days. Another summer passed but I was not going back to the Alps or to British rock until hands and feet were finished: a light-hearted but abortive seasonal sally to Glencoe which ended in whisky and wheelchairs in Glasgow Infirmary on New Year's Day effectively convinced me of the futility of more active anticipation. Finally, however, last May, the time arrived, the tailoring and testing on pavement and corridor was over and we drove north to Scotland on a new day. Michael Williams stepped off the train at Bridge of Orchy, the Black Mount was behind us, and there was the Buachaille standing like a trumpet call across the moor; clouds wheeled up to the summit and I had bright new stubby brown boots winking at me on my feet. It was a good day, a day absorbed with the rock, for my wife also was learning to climb. How to do it was all-important and sufficient too on my favourite mountain with the warmth of old associations close about me. We moved on, and over the following days the permutations, doubts and hopes of this new climbing were worked out. It was a question of finding the right combination, just as it had been before, and while I was learning there wasn't time for other questions.

Before long, however, as I began to find my new limit, I noticed more and more strongly a sensation of what I can only describe as disharmony with the mountain. It started as an odd restlessness, a growing unhappiness which was present even when I was climbing, and it became stronger and stronger until I realised with a shock that I was losing the old feeling of well-being which came through merely being in the mountains and I had almost lost the joy of climbing itself. It was not the restlessness which I found when I first came to the hills and which ended when I began to climb: that had had a certainty of eventual solution; this, on the contrary, was a growing uncertainty. There was a finality about it like a new road that suddenly ends in the middle of a moor. There's a cluster of deserted huts on wheels and a jumble of dead machinery and that's all; you have to go back, but I couldn't go back.

I knew what the trouble was: over the last few days I had found how I would have to climb in future; my new limits were defined. I found no difficulty in accepting that. I had already accepted it three years before, but with these limitations I could now no longer achieve the relationship with mountains that I had found before. I had lost two things: first was the intense physical enjoyment of the climb, the touch of the rock itself, warm granite crinkling under my fingers, the splendid certainty of pulling up over the bulging rock or swinging out on the hand traverse. These were simple physical freedoms, but with them had gone the ability to extend myself on the mountain. I now had to climb cautiously, there was little in reserve, and because of this the second, the important, loss had occurred. My discovery of myself, and those intense moments of happiness which were the unique gift of the mountain, which informed my harmony with mountains, had been founded on a creed of intense action. The latter was denied me so the former was lost. So my thoughts went round and round in a tight little circle as we left Glencoe and Nevis to drive north to the Sutherland hills. I could see the only answer, it required very little imagination to realise what it must be, but I could not believe in it. The act of acceptance eluded me; eluded, that is, until the day on Stack Polly which I described at the beginning.

I don't want to give the impression that I made a conscious act of will on that ledge of the tower. I did not say to myself 'I believe' nor did I cry

'Eureka' and spring to the summit. But when I took the weight of the man on my shoulders I was forced to strike hard against the mountain with all my strength, and in that moment I found the physical conflict which I thought I had lost. To touch the mountain was grace, yes, but to take hold of it, to wrestle with it, to hear that shouting surge of the spirit which came in the moment of attack on storm slopes of ice or rock, this was what had been held from me. For a brief time I could engage the mountain with all my strength, and when the moment passed I found that with the recognition of this hunger its pangs had abated. I had already arrived at an intellectual assessment of my situation, but I had not accepted it emotionally because I had not completely explored my loss in terms of emotional need; now that I was confronted by it, however, I could define and accept it, and acceptance was softened by the realisation that this appetite could still be satisfied in unexpected ways.

For the rest of that day I was happy, for I was moving in my own country once more; it was a springing happiness which I have continued to feel whenever I have been in the mountains since then, whatever I am doing, whether climbing an easy route or one which taxes my present ability, such as it is, to the limit. Now this simply used not to happen, for although I could find intense happiness in the hills, I was restless and felt vaguely cheated and disappointed if weather or other circumstance forced us to have an easy day. A change must have occurred, the old unrestrained curiosity had gone, and something less limited had taken its place. I don't mean by this that I simply wanted to walk in the valley. Climbing was still important and I wanted to climb as well as I could, but it was not necessary to take it to excess. The simple act of ascending was enough; I could draw my strength from the hills without a desperate beating on their sides. That this was so I proved to my own satisfaction when we returned to the Alps in July.

We spent three weeks in Zermatt; it was my fourth Alpine season and I can say without hesitation that I enjoyed it as much as any of the preceding ones. There was the old thrill of crampons biting into hard snow, the glacier before dawn, clouds racing up from Italy and the new thrill of being able to hold an ice axe by the head with one hand; the old half-forgotten uncertainty on steep loose snow and icy rock of my first season, ending in the same rush of pleasure as confidence returned, and the new uncertainty of climbing on steep ice. There was no hesitancy, nothing was blurred; the impressions were sharp and clear, changing with each route. These, however, were the initial quantities of the equation, through them the beauty was as intense, my friends had not changed, but what of the final result of all these factors, the special attitudes of mind which mountains confer?

Originally, the first of these, I suppose, was the attraction of mountains when I first saw them. Tyndall attributed this to 'the forgotten associations of a far-gone ancestry'; I can only hiccup in astonishment. Any attempt to extend that argument would end in farce. No, I can only think that it was chiefly the impact of a new and infinitely challenging beauty. The challenge was the unknown in the mountain and myself, and it could only be resolved by climbing and continuing to climb; the beauty always remained. There was, however, another element in this first attraction: mountains have always been obvious and convenient natural symbols and certainly I realise now that they were symbolic for me when I first saw them, not in any definitely accepted religious sense but in a way which I shall return to in a moment.

When I had actually started to climb, the initial time was busy with the mechanics of the new world, with the exhilarating novelty of the beauty seen from a different angle, with the new friendships, and all this compounded the attraction of the hills at that period. Later, when I came to the harder routes, I found something else, a new state of mind which I have mentioned briefly already. This was a sudden and overwhelmingly powerful sensation of humility and gratitude, so real that I could only interpret it as being directed towards a creator. I had never been able to arrive at such a conviction through a process of reason, yet here I was forced to accept it, despite myself, through the very certainty and intensity of these emotions. There was no element of pantheism in my interpretation; my emotions strongly implied the personality and the transcendence of the Creator. I can only define such experience by using the word *mystical*; it is, I imagine, a manifestation of nature-mysticism: my particular relationship with the mountain, the natural order, had resulted in a profound apprehension of a transcendent order. It was the knowledge of God in his creatures, Eckhart's evening light. I would emphasise that the first time this experience was manifest I had made no conscious effort to achieve it; there was no act of contemplation. It just happened when I was coiling up the rope at the end of a climb; as prosaic as that. Afterwards, however, I sought it again and again, but my mistake, some might call it a heresy, was to approach it through difficulty because this had been the relationship with the natural object which had led to its first manifestation. I could only find it with certainty through longer, more exacting expeditions. This was the naïvety of approach which I spoke of earlier. Charles Meade has rightly condemned it when he says 'an intensification of technique is not a reliable means for sustaining a mystical reaction', and more severely: 'A sense of unity with nature is one of the principal characteristics in nature-mysticism, whereas the desire for adventure in its extreme form is the absorbing preoccupation, not of the nature-mystic but of the danger-mystic who takes to danger as a stimulant.' I must confess to having enjoyed the stimulant occasionally, and I don't suppose any member of this club could honestly say that he had never done so, but its real importance for me was to arrive at what is the same purpose as the nature-mystic's. I was employing the wrong means for what I still consider to be the right end.

Nowadays I no longer need to sharpen sensibility on the whetstone of danger. When I see the hills I see them in their old beauty and I see my friends and myself upon them, as we are now and as we have been. When

I walk and climb, awareness is present on the bye-days as on the days of endeavour. It is still evening light, but perhaps the light will grow stronger in time.

Having said this, and probably having firmly established in your minds the picture of a monomaniac setting off intrepidly into the hills with his butterfly net in search of extra-sensory Lepidoptera, I should like briefly to look at perhaps the oddest and oldest question of all: 'Why do I like going uphill?' Mummery said, 'I am free to confess that I myself should still climb, even though there were no scenery to look at'. I would take this perhaps beyond Mummery's meaning to assert that I would still climb even if there was no view and no technical difficulty, nothing except the simple movement upwards. To explain this feeling I have to go back to my earliest days. Throughout childhood, in the books, in the stories that one read, hills nearly always figured as symbols of a better life. The prince and his princess, the toy soldier and the match girl, they all went over the hill to happiness. My favourite line in Beatrix Potter was 'Over the hills and far away she danced with Pigling Bland'. Later, at school, the road to London went over the hill, and the summer holiday in Wales ended when we rounded the corner and the hills shut out the view, so that it was not surprising that hills must always have had lingering traces of a romantic affinity with the better life. It is these affinities which must partially explain this odd satisfaction in walking uphill, these and the accumulated experience of our mountain lives which does in fact prove that there is a better life to be found in hills. I see it, then, as an expression of a natural optimism which is both romantic and founded in reality. Optimism may come close to William James' definition of mysticism, but I prefer to leave it at that; anything more would put me perilously near emulating that splendid hero of J.B. Morton's who pushed a pebble with his nose all the way to the top of the mountain.

PHOTOGRAPHS AND ILLUSTRATIONS

The members of the expedition. *Top row (left to right):* Johar, Rustam. *Middle row (left to right):* Nadil, Sahib Shah, Scott Hamilton, Rae Culbert, Shakoor Beg, Nadir. *Bottom row (left to right):* Dhilap Shah, Bernard Jillott, Tony Streather, John Emery.

1 Tony Streather
2 Bernard Jillott
3 Scott Hamilton
4 John Emery
5 Rae Culbert

The north face of Haramosh,
showing the summit on the right.

Looking up into the icefall
from Camp II.

Looking up towards the north-east ridge from Camp III. The left-to-right 'retroussé' slope in the middle distance was the route to Camp IV.

The fluted ridge on the far side of the Haramosh glacier, showing a typical 'bergschrund' at the change of levels.

Looking down at Camp IV. Immediately below the camp is the narrow neck of snow and the crevasse into which Emery fell. Beyond is the slope down to the Haramosh glacier.

Nearing the north-east ridge. The track bends to the left over the snow bridge crossing the crevasse in the foreground and then winds up towards the ice cliffs to the right of the Cardinal's hat.

On the north-east ridge, showing the start of the steep slope down into the trough. Straight ahead is one of the peaks of Haramosh II.

'Come on up! You can't imagine what you'll see when you get here.'

Jillott and Emery setting
off for the Cardinal's hat.

Streather and Emery crossing the snow
slope below the La on the way down.

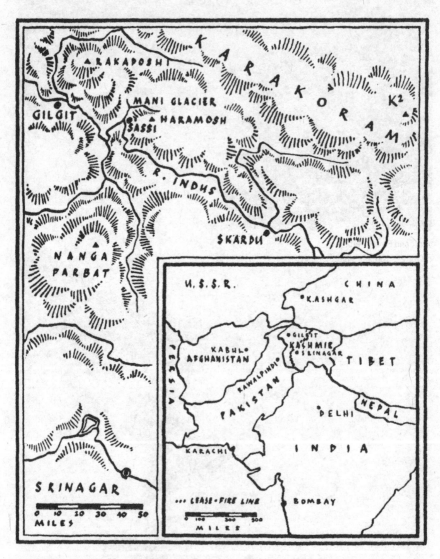

Sketch map of the Karakoram and District.

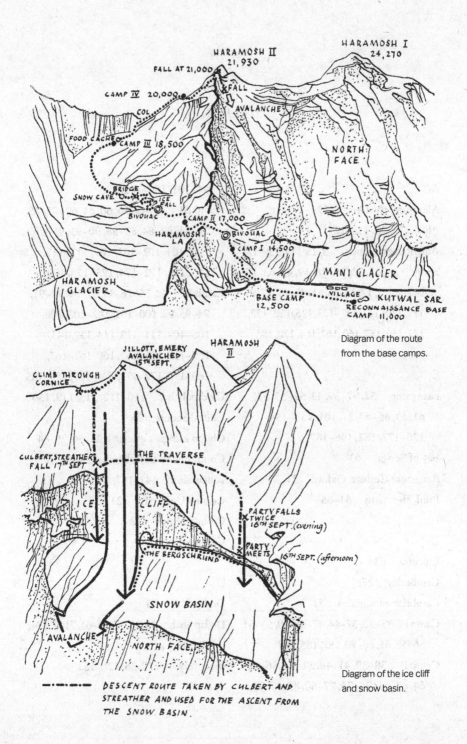

Diagram of the route from the base camps.

Diagram of the ice cliff and snow basin.

INDEX

Printed in the USA
CPSIA information can be obtained
at www.ICGtesting.com
JSHW031705140824
68134JS00037B/3528

9 781912 560424